Digital

Printmaking

Digital Printmaking

GEORGE WHALE
& NAREN BARFIELD

WATSON-GUPTILL PUBLICATIONS/NEW YORK

Copyright © 2001, 2003 George Whale & Naren Barfield

First published in the United States in 2003 by
Watson-Guptill Publications
770 Broadway
New York, NY 10003
www.watson-guptill.com

Cover design by Dorothy Moir
Designed by Keith Watson

Library of Congress Control Number: 2002109813

ISBN 0-8230-1398-7

First published in Great Britain 2001
A & C Black (Publishers) Limited
37 Soho Square, London W1D 3QZ
www.acblack.com

Front cover illustration: *Study IV for The Shadow*, Raz Barfield, UK, 1996.
Back cover illustration: *Space and Space/Nature - 95E*, Susumu Endo, Japan, 1995.

Printed in Malaysia by Times Offset (M) Sdn. Bhd.
First printing, 2003
1 2 3 4 5 6 / 07 06 05 04 03

CONTENTS

DEDICATION

This book is dedicated to the memory of Tristan Humphries, a pioneer of digital printmaking who opened doors for other artists.

The Journey, Tristan Humphries, UK, 1995. One of a series of inkjet prints made as part of the *Computers, Print Technology, and Printmaking* research project, which was set up by Tristan in 1994 at Camberwell College of Arts, London, and Chelsea College of Art and Design, London. (Courtesy of Karyn White.)

ACKNOWLEDGEMENTS

The authors would like to thank all of the artists who submitted work for consideration and the manufacturers, suppliers and editioning studios who offered advice or provided images for inclusion in the book. Special thanks are due to Paul Coldwell for his work in the early stages of the project, and to Raz Barfield for his constructive and expert advice. Also to Heather Hoover for her knowledge of toner transfer process, to Sasha Grishin for introducing us to Australian printmakers and finally to Michelle Tiernan and Linda Lambert of A & C Black for their unwavering support.

Notes for readers in the United States

The following are US equivalents of terms mentioned in this book:

bureaux: commercial printers
DIY: do-it-yourself
graphics bureau: graphics house

The Studio March 28th 1995, David Hockney, UK, 1995. Iris inkjet print on Somerset paper, 89 x 111cm (35 x 43.7in.). Printed by Nash Editions, Manhattan Beach, CA.

INTRODUCTION

In recent years we have witnessed the development of some remarkable technologies that defy conventional categorisation yet enable artists to create prints of a technical quality comparable to the highest standards of traditional etchings, engravings, block-prints, screenprints and lithographs. These new types of prints have one thing in common – they owe their existence to digital computers, whose evolution during the last two decades from monolithic calculating machines into powerful and affordable devices for the creation and manipulation of pictures has presented artists with fresh creative opportunities.

Graphical computing not only offers new techniques for combining and manipulating images, and for speedily turning creative ideas into prints, but also enables printmakers to access and utilise many different sources. Drawings, paintings and photographs; poetry, music and dance; CAT-scans, mathematical models and computational processes – all can be represented

The Internalized Page Project Vol. 2: The Character Exhibition, Charles Long, USA, 1998. Iris print, 27.9 x 21.6cm (11 x 8.5in.). One of a boxed set of seven prints. Line drawings on legal paper were transformed into three-dimensional computer models. Printed by Muse [X] Editions, Los Angeles.

symbolically in digital form and are, in principle, interchangeable. Far from being 'just another tool', the computer enables traditional media to be integrated with new kinds of ideas and imagery, potentially dissolving the boundaries between printmaking and other forms of artistic and scientific expression.

Many of the world's most prestigious art galleries and institutions count digital prints in their collections. This success is largely the result of artistic collaborations initiated by a handful

Fragment, Barbara Robertson, USA, 2000. Inkjet, collagraph, and photocopy transfer on Somerset paper, 53.3 x 43.2cm (21 x 17in.). (Courtesy of Davidson Galleries, Seattle.) A collagraph was printed on top of an inkjet print in an etching press and, once dry, a black and white photocopy was transferred to the surface. This print is one of a set of three *Urban Botanicals*, mixed media prints standing as 'metaphors of the relationship between nature and technology.'

Index of Possibilities (Ping-Feng), Milan Milojevic, Australia, 1999. Layered inkjet on Stonehenge paper, 42 x 60cm (16.5 x 23.6in.). One of a series of prints of animal 'hybrids' derived from illustrations in Konrad Gesner's 16th-century *Historia Animalium*, and corresponding to the fanciful creatures described in Jorge Luis Borges' *The Book of Imaginary Beings*.

of professional editioning studios (notably Cone Editions Press, Adamson Editions, and Nash Editions, all based in the US), whose foresight and ingenuity enabled them to identify and exploit the printmaking possibilities of modern, electronic pre-press devices – notably the Scitex Iris printer – and to make innovations of their own, raising levels of quality and durability. At the same time, artists worldwide have continued to exercise their imaginations in adapting all kinds of computer technologies for creative use. Some have adopted 'all-digital' approaches, in which the output of a digital device such as a desktop laser printer, or an inkjet printer, is the finished print, whilst others have devised 'hybrid' techniques inventively combining digital output – film positives, machined metal plates, even tracings or memories of displayed images – with traditional media. This pioneering spirit endures, transforming and re-energising the art and craft of printmaking, and challenging some long-held assumptions about the nature and status of the fine print.

Two things, at least, remain constant: firstly, many artists remain committed to the idea of the print as a physical object, something that can be held in the hand, or hung on the wall; secondly, despite several decades of effort in the field of Artificial Intelligence (AI), human creativity remains paramount, and the prospect of a print conceived and produced entirely

Conjura (Conjuration), Rafael Rivera-Rosa, Puerto Rico, 1999. Inkjet on Arches watercolour paper, 35.6 x 35.6 cm (14 x 14in.).

by computer is still a long way off.

This handbook will show some of the exciting and imaginative ways in which artists from all over the world are currently utilising computers in their work. We hope that their example will stimulate other artists and students to arm themselves with a little basic computer knowledge and to explore some of the ideas and techniques for themselves, so that they too can take advantage of the tremendous opportunities for innovation in the field of digital printmaking.

Chapters 1 to 4 present a practical introduction to 'all-digital' printmaking, reviewing the different kinds of digital images, the computer programs used to create and manipulate them, and the devices used to output them. There is advice on how to set up and run a digital studio, a step-by-step guide to making an archival-quality editioned print and

Event Horizon, Phillip George, Australia,1997. Electrostatic prints on canvas, and acrylic, 120 x 288cm (47.2 x 113.4in.).

Ursula, Dorothy Simpson Krause, USA, 1998. Digital collage, 89 x 71cm (35 x 28in.). One of a series inspired by *Macomber House*, a collection of poems by Ray Amorosi. A reverse image, printed on Rexam clear film, was burnished onto a spray-dampened fresco panel. The 'frame', consisting of the same image printed on gold paper, was aligned and adhered with PVA.

coverage of advanced techniques.

Chapters 5 and 6, aimed at experienced printmakers and students of printmaking, show some of the exciting ways in which computer technologies have been integrated with traditional forms of printmaking including relief, intaglio, screenprinting and lithography; how digital images can be used to make plates, screens and blocks, and how software can extend the print-maker's 'visual vocabulary'.

Chapter 7 looks at the work of digital ateliers and their use of large-format (i.e. wide-format) printers to produce editions of the very

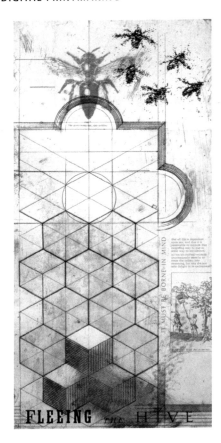

Fleeing the Hive, Lisa A. Moline, USA, 1990. Dot-matrix printing with intaglio and letterpress, 76.2 x 35.6cm (30 x 14in.). A print combining traditional and digital techniques: etching, aquatint and drypoint (main structure), intaglio photocopy transfer (orange queen bee), letterpress (text and beekeeper), four-colour dot-matrix (bees at top and cloudy swarm at bottom-right).

highest professional standards. There is also advice on how to prepare work for output by commercial print bureaux.

Chapter 8 describes work by print artists who have broken free of the limitations of commercial software by writing their own, adapting ideas from fields as diverse as genetics and scientific visualisation to produce some of the most interesting work currently on view.

Chapter 9 considers the future of printmaking in a digital world, with particular reference to the Internet.

The Glossary explains many of the terms relating specifically to digital printmaking.

The Bibliography lists a number of books covering particular aspects of digital imaging and printing. Additional sources are listed under Supplies and Services and Other Information Sources.

Chapter 1
THE DIGITAL STUDIO

All that is required to become a proficient computer user is a little time and effort and, of course, access. Small computer systems are of two main types: PC (IBM-compatible personal computer) and Mac® (Apple® Macintosh® computer). Most things can be done on both types of computers, but it seems that most artists favour the Mac.

As well as the computer itself, equipment is needed to get images into it, and to print images out. One of the most useful devices for inputting images is a *scanner*, which can sample full-colour images so that they can be viewed, stored, accessed, and manipulated. The most popular types of printers are *laser printers* and *inkjet printers*, both are able to produce high-quality black and white or colour output onto paper and film.

Computers usually come with a monitor (screen) for viewing, a keyboard for typing, and a small device called a mouse with one or two buttons on top. Whenever the mouse is moved, a small pointer moves across the screen, enabling the user to interact with the computer simply by pointing and clicking. All of the input devices (keyboard, mouse, scanner) and output devices (monitor, printer) are connected by cable to the main computer unit, a box with slots at the front and sockets at the back or side.

Programs (also known as *software*) are the sets of instructions that transform the computer from a costly paperweight into a useful tool. The main program in any computer is the operating system (OS), which automatically controls and coordinates its activities: the Mac uses versions of the Mac OS (e.g. Mac OS 9, Mac OS X); PCs use the Windows® operating system (e.g. Windows 98, Windows 2000). Then there are the driver programs that control the scanner, printer, and other devices. Finally, there are the applications – programs designed for particular tasks, like typing letters, building databases or, more importantly, making and manipulating images. The next chapter will look at application software in more detail, but first the equipment, or *hardware*.

The computer

Here's a fairly typical specification for a stand-alone (i.e. non-networked) PC or Mac system suitable for digital printmaking:

17-inch non-interlaced colour monitor

A monitor with a sharp, flicker-free screen is essential and should be able to display full colour at high resolutions.

At least 128 MB of RAM

RAM is the computer's memory, where programs and images are stored whilst in use; the more RAM there is (as measured in MB, or *megabytes*), the faster images can be loaded and edited. The system should have plenty of scope for upgrading RAM later on.

Internal hard disk drive, at least 5 GB (*gigabytes*)

The hard disk is the computer's permanent memory, where software and image *files* are saved. Large image files can quickly fill the disk so, as with RAM, the bigger the better.

Processor

The microprocessor chip (e.g. G3 or G4 for Macintosh or Pentium® III processor for PC) is the computer's 'brain'. In general, a processor with a high 'clock speed' (measured in MHz, or megaHertz) is better than one with a low clock speed, but other factors are equally important in determining the performance of the system.

Built-in Zip/Jaz drive

Zip® cartridges are widely used for 'backing-up' work – copying it from the hard disk for storage elsewhere – and for transporting work from one computer to another, as when taking print files to a bureau for output. Zips are compatible with both PC and Mac, and come in two sizes – 100 MB and 250 MB – sufficient for storing scores of images. Zip cartridges need a Zip drive to slot into, which can be external (attached to the computer by a cable) or supplied as part of the main unit. Jaz® cartridges and drives are similar to Zips, only with greater capacity – 1 GB or 2 GB – especially useful for very large image files.

Built-in CD-ROM (or DVD) drive

Many photo-processing outlets are able to convert slides and photos to digital images, putting them onto inexpensive CDs. To read CDs containing software or images, a computer should either have a built-in CD drive or one of the newer DVD (Digital Versatile Disk) drives, which can read standard CDs as well as DVDs.

Mouse and keyboard

A keyboard (used mainly for typing in text) and mouse (for pointing and clicking) are usually provided as standard with any desktop system.

Internal modem

A modem allows for Internet connection through a telephone line, giving access to electronic mail (email) and the World Wide Web (www).

Scanners

Flatbed scanners are able to make reflective scans from opaque originals or, with a suitable adaptor, transmissive scans from transparencies. Low-cost scanners, manufactured by Agfa, Heidelberg, Umax and others, use arrays of tiny light detectors called charge-coupled devices (CCDs) to convert reflected light from an image into digital form, a grid of coloured dots (picture elements, or *pixels*). The key factors are scanning area, optical *resolution*, typically 600 x 1200 *ppi* (pixels per inch) or 1200 x 2400 ppi, and dynamic range – the range of tones that can be captured. A successful scan should retain detail in highlight and shadow areas, and capture subtle variations of tone and colour. As with other peripherals, it is important to ensure that a scanner is compatible with the computer, and that its driver software is installed on the computer. Many scanners have a locking system, used during transportation – be sure to unlock before use.

The Umax® Astra 3450 is an inexpensive flatbed colour scanner that plugs into the USB port of a Mac or PC. Up to 21.6 x 29.7cm (8.5 x 11.7in.) for reflective scans, up to 12.7 x 10.2cm (5 x 4in.) for transparencies.

Printers

The range of digital printers and related technologies used by printmakers is large, and growing (see Table 1, page 20), but by far the most popular devices for home and studio are laser printers and inkjet printers.

Laser printers

The laser printer uses a laser beam to create a positive electrostatic image on a drum which (as in a photocopier) picks up negatively-charged toner and transfers it to paper, where it is fused to the surface by heat and pressure. The resolution of a laser printer is typically 600 or 1200 *dpi* (dots per inch). In colour lasers, four passes are performed, transferring cyan, magenta, yellow and black toners to the page one at a time, or first creating the four-colour image on an intermediate surface. Laser printers produce consistent results with different types of paper; cost per print is mainly determined by the cost of toner cartridges (recycled ones can often be much cheaper than new ones).

Inkjet printers

Inkjet printing is a non-contact process whereby an image is built up from droplets of ink (usually water-based) sprayed from fine nozzles mounted on a print head, which scans the paper. In continuous inkjet (CIJ), used in Iris large-format printers, high-pressure pumps force the inks through nozzles in continuous streams of tiny droplets; unwanted droplets are electrically charged and deflected away, whilst the remainder strike the *substrate*, combining to form variable-sized dots on the surface, and giving near *continuous-tone* quality.

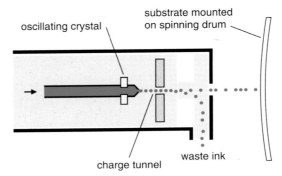

Continuous flow inkjet. Pressurised ink is broken into fine droplets by a rapidly oscillating crystal. The droplets pass through a charge tunnel, where the unwanted ones are given an electrical charge, deflecting them away from the substrate.

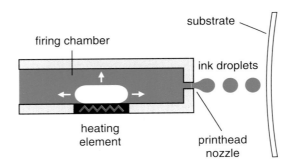

Thermal inkjet printing. Whenever a dot is required, an electrical pulse to a tiny heating element creates a bubble of vapour whose rapid expansion forces ink out of the nozzle. When the element is switched off and cools down, fresh ink is drawn back in. The printhead contains hundreds of these hair-fine nozzles for each ink colour.

Epson® Stylus® Photo 870. This A4 piezo inkjet printer incorporates six-colour variable-sized droplet technology, and prints at 1440 x 720 dpi (dots per inch) on a range of papers. There is a 10-year lightfastness guarantee with recommended materials.

More common, and less expensive, are drop-on-demand (DOD) inkjet printers (usually four-colour, sometimes six or more) made by Canon, EnCAD, Epson, Hewlett-Packard and others, in formats from *A4* (8.4 x 11.9in.) up to *A0* (33.6 x 47.5in.) and beyond, and resolutions up to 1440 x 1440 dpi or more. Each ink droplet is ejected when needed, either by the action of an element that heats the ink to create a tiny pressure bubble (thermal inkjet, or bubblejet), or by a piezo-electric crystal (piezo inkjet). The piezo process allows more control over dot size and shape, and has driven the development of ultra micro dot (UMD) and variable-sized droplet (VSD) technologies, which can improve not only resolution, but also colour, since the ability to combine tiny drops in different amounts effectively creates a larger palette of solid colours.

A Roland Hi-Fi JET 1440 dpi large-format piezo inkjet printer.

Table 1: Output technologies used in printmaking (with examples of manufacturing companies)

TECHNOLOGY	MANUFACTURERS	DESCRIPTION
Airbrush printing	Signtech, Vutek, Belcom	Ink or paint, under air pressure, is directed at the surface through traversing spray heads, controlled by electromagnetic valves. Used for relatively low-resolution, grand-format (ultra-large) printing on all kinds of substrates.
CNC (computer-numerically controlled) cutting	GCC, Roland	Machinery cuts film material, often self-adhesive vinyl, for making large-format exterior signs from vector-based images.
CNC engraving	Pacer, Gold, Kern	Direct engraving into blocks or sheet materials. Fine detail possible, especially with laser engravers. Can be used to make matrices for relief/intaglio printing.
CNC routing	Gerber, Shoda	Direct cutting into wood, plastic, foamboard and metal materials in large formats, up to two or more inches deep.
Computer-to-plate	Dupont	Images transferred directly from computer to very fast photo-litho plates using blue laser scanning technology. Used in commercial printing.
Dot-matrix printing	Brother, Epson, Lexmark	Made obsolescent by inkjet and laser, dot-matrix printing builds an image from dots made by tiny pins striking an inked ribbon in contact with paper. Small-format, poor resolution and quality, unsuitable for colour printing.
Dye-sublimation	Kodak, Tektronix, Mitsubishi	Solid inks on rolls of film are heated to high temperature, converting them into gas which impregnates special paper. Dot size can be varied by controlling the temperature, giving images of almost photographic quality. Small- to medium-format, expensive consumables.
Electrostatic printing	Xerox, Rastergraphics	Specially treated paper passes over an electrically-charged head, where the image area is given a positive charge; negatively-charged toner particles attach to the image area, and are fused to the paper. Large-format, medium resolution, poor resistance to moisture and abrasion.
Film recorder (slide writer)	Polaroid, Lasergraphics	Device used by bureaux to transfer digital images directly to film, so they can be enlarged and printed photographically.
Imagesetting	Linotype-Hell, Scitex	Thermal or laser device for producing very high resolution (2400 dpi or more) monochromatic halftones or line art on film or bromide.
Inkjet, continuous (CIJ)	Scitex Iris	Fine nozzles under continuous pressure issue a stream of ink droplets; unwanted droplets are given an electrical charge and deflected away from the substrate. Low print speed (up to an hour for a large print), near-photographic quality printing on large-format coated and uncoated art papers of any weight.
Inkjet, drop-on-demand (DOD)	Epson, Hewlett-Packard, Canon, Xerox, Lexmark, EnCAD, Kodak, ColorSpan, Roland	Droplets of ink are ejected from nozzles as required. In thermal (bubblejet) printers, a heating element generates the ejection pressure; piezo inkjet systems use piezo-electric pressure. All formats from small to

grand, resolutions up to 1440 dpi and more. Broad range of special substrates available, and many printers can print onto heavy art papers.

Inkjet, solid ('phase-change')	Tektronix	Ink is in the form of solid wax sticks. The wax is liquified before being sprayed onto a transfer drum, from where it is cold-fused onto the paper in one pass. Resolution up to around 850 x 450 dpi, up to A3 format, vibrant colour on all papers, poor permanence. Designed for near-continuous usage.
Laminated object manufacturing (LOM)	Helisys, CAM-LEM	Software converts 3D computer model into sectional profiles, which are laser-cut from sheet material and bonded to create a solid block of laminate. Used for rapid prototyping of designed objects.
Laser imaging	Durst, CSI	Use of red, green, and blue lasers to transfer digital images directly onto colour photo-graphic material, in large and grand formats.
Laser printing	Canon, Xerox, Elite, Hewlett-Packard	A scanning laser beam is used to create an electrostatic image on a revolving, photo-receptive drum. Exposed areas of the drum pick up charged toner powder and transfer it to paper or film. Resolution typically 600 or 1200 dpi, formats A4 and A3.
LED printing and LCD printing	Oki, IBM	Similar to laser printing, but potentially cheaper and with fewer moving parts. Uses a matrix of LEDs (light-emitting diodes) to expose the drum. Mainly for high-volume printing. Similarly, LCD printing exposes the drum by shining a light through a liquid crystal display (LCD) panel.
Pen-plotting	Roland, EnCAD, Ioline	Flatbed or drum device in which a moving head holding a pen draws lines on paper or film up to A0 dimensions. Plotters have been adapted for etching by replacing the pen with an inscribing point. (Now obsolescent.)
Pictrography	Fuji	Laser diodes expose a sensitive donor paper to which heat and moisture are applied to create a dye image, which is transferred to receptor paper or film. Small-format, photo-quality colour.
Screen projection		Commercial process for directly exposing screen photo-stencil by laser.
Stereolithography	Aaroflex, Donken	Relief surfaces or solid objects built from photopolymer layers, selectively hardened by laser scanning.The cured surface can be abraded, machined, and polished.
Thermal transfer printing	Tektronix, Océ	Rolls of plastic film coated with coloured wax or resin (CMY, CMYK, sometimes spot colour), which is melted, one colour at a time, on contact with paper. Intense, uniform colour, good moisture resistance. Small-formats, low resolution.
Thermo autochrome printing	Fuji, Panasonic	Special paper containing three layers of pigment (CMY), each sensitive to a particular temperature, is passed beneath a thermal/UV head three times, heat-activating then UV-fixing a single colour each time. Mainly used for small-format printing in conjunction with digital cameras.

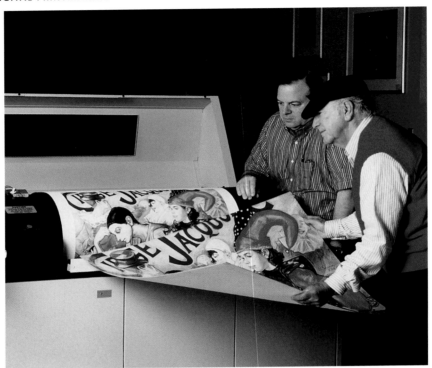

Hunter Editions of Kennebunkport, Maine, USA, are specialists in fine art *giclée* printmaking. Here, Michael H. Brown (President) and artist Shelley Schoneberg (in hat) inspect a print from an Iris printer. (Photograph courtesy of Hunter Editions.)

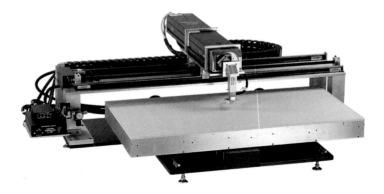

Laser cutting and engraving system, by Kern Electronics & Lasers Inc. The table size is 122 x 61cm (48 x 24in.). Engraving speeds can reach up to 76cm (30in.) per minute, and the spot size of the laser beam can be adjusted by using different lenses. Digital images supplied in standard formats (e.g. TIFF, AutoCAD or CorelDRAW files) can be laser engraved into virtually any non-metal, though hard, fine-grained woods tend to give the best results. (Photograph courtesy of Kern Electronics & Lasers Inc.)

Pen-plotter. US artist
Roman Verostko
mixes his own ink
colours, and has also
adapted oriental
brushes to fit the
plotter's drawing
arm. (Photograph
courtesy of Roman
Verostko.)

Other useful equipment

Slide scanner
A dedicated slide scanner will produce higher quality scans of 35mm (or
other format) transparencies than a slide adaptor on a conventional
flatbed scanner.

Digital camera
Digital cameras have conventional optics but, like scanners, use CCD
technology to capture an image. Dozens, or hundreds of images can be
compressed and saved on a memory card and directly downloaded to the
computer. Affordable digital cameras have fairly low resolution – from 640
x 480 pixels to around 1500 x 1000 pixels, not as high as that possible from
a scan of a photographic print or slide.

The Intuos® 4x5 from Wacom® is a compact, pressure-sensitive tablet and pen (stylus) for interactive drawing and painting.

Tablet and stylus

As an alternative to the mouse, a pressure-sensitive tablet used in conjunction with a pen-like stylus allows for far more controllable interactive drawing, tracing and painting. Some styli are sensitive to tilt and bearing.

CD writer

Files stored on magnetic media such as hard disks and Zip disks can deteriorate after only a few years. Permanent archives are best stored on CDs, and for this a CD writer is needed. A CD can hold 650 MB, and can be written in 'hybrid' form enabling it to be read on both PC and Mac.

Gaining access

Before spending upwards of UK£1000 (US$1430) on a computer, scanner and printer, it's worth doing some research, as the technology is continually changing. Many educational facilities and public-access print workshops now have well-equipped digital imaging and print studios where it is possible to learn and experiment with new technology. Websites devoted to printmaking (see Other Information Sources, page 124) may include information about digital techniques, and artists and printers themselves are sometimes highly knowledgeable about hardware and at the

The digital studio: photographer Andy Stewart (UK) and Billy (UK) take a break whilst awaiting a printout. Their imaging and printing system fits comfortably in a corner, and has everything needed for making small prints, or for proofing prior to large-format bureau output. The set-up comprises: a Power Macintosh G3 computer, with 17 inch display, keyboard, and mouse; A3 inkjet printer (lower shelf); Zip drive (on top of the blue computer unit) for storing images on disk; and a scanner (far right), used to input photographs and drawings. (Photographed by Andy Whale Photography, London, using a Nikon Coolpix 990 digital camera.)

very least, an artist considering working in this field should first acquire some basic graphical computing skills, perhaps by attending an introductory course in Adobe Photoshop at a local college or adult education centre.

Buying tips

Having decided what is required, it is time to shop around for an affordable system matching the specification. Substantial discounts can often be obtained from mail order outlets, but there are potential pitfalls (magazines for Mac and PC users offer advice to direct buyers; some also run mail order protection schemes for readers). Whether ordering from a retailer, or directly, it is important first of all to:

• confirm that the proposed system will be able to do what it's intended for; for example, if the intention is to make inkjet prints onto heavy papers, make sure that the printer will be able to cope;

• remember to budget for software and consumables; if there's any money left over, go for a better monitor, more RAM, or a faster processor;

• obtain written details of the terms of deliveries, warranties, and technical support; find out if the servicing agreement is on-site or back-to-base;

• ensure that all the necessary cables, driver software and manuals are included;

• arrange home/studio insurance for the equipment.

And after delivery:

• notify the supplier straight away if anything is missing or broken;

• complete and return any hardware/software warranty forms;

• ensure that the equipment is secure; make a note of the model and serial number of each item, and keep it in a safe place.

Health and safety

Manuals should always be consulted for health and safety information. However, the following guidelines are generally applicable:

• the monitor should be placed on a secure surface at a comfortable reading distance and, to avoid eye strain, shielded from glare;

• hands and wrists should be supported whilst typing at the keyboard (ergonomic keyboards and hand-rests are available);

• the position and height of chair and desktop should be adjusted to minimise twisting or hunching, which can cause back or neck problems;

• printers should be installed in a well-ventilated area (especially lasers, as they emit ozone);

• when working at the computer, take regular breaks, at least five minutes every fifteen – twenty minutes;

• do not attempt to repair the monitor – it can deliver a huge electric shock even when unplugged; in any case, DIY repairs can invalidate warranties.

Chapter 2
WORKING WITH DIGITAL IMAGES

■ Computers require that every image, whether it be a photograph, a drawing or a single brushstroke, is represented as numbers. Instead of using the familiar, decimal numbers which everyone can understand, computers use binary numbers. These are made up of binary digits (*bits* – zeros and ones), which is why computer images are often referred to as *digital images*. Fortunately, all of the complicated 'number-crunching' that goes on whenever a digital image is being made or modified is taken care of by programs, leaving the artist free to concentrate on being creative.

Some graphics/imaging programs are supplied with the computer, but most are bought on CD, with instructions telling the buyer what types of computer it can be used with, how to install it, and how to use it once it's installed. 'Demo' applications, obtained free with magazines, or downloaded from the Internet, are often useful in deciding what to buy. For those who baulk at the idea of actual payment, there is also 'freeware' – fully functional programs that cost nothing (and may or may not work as intended). Shareware – try before you buy – is also available.

Digital images can be created from scratch or derived from an existing image such as a drawing or a photograph. There are different types of images, and different applications for working with them; many have been successfully utilised by printmakers.

Digital painting
Applications: Corel® Painter™, Pixel Paint Pro, AppleWorks®, Windows Paint.

Painting applications make it possible to use a mouse or stylus for freehand drawing and painting.

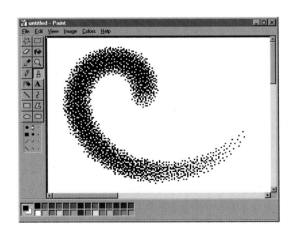

Graphical user interface (GUI) of a simple paint application (Microsoft Paint). 'Zoomed' view of a single, interactively-drawn brushmark shows the pixel structure.

Lip Service, Laurence Gartel, USA, 1986. Cibachrome print of a MacPaint image, 27.9 x 21.6cm (11 x 8.5in.).

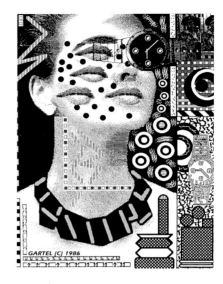

The figure on the previous page shows the graphical interface that appears on screen when running Paint, an application that comes pre-installed with Windows PCs. There is a horizontal menu at the top, a small 'palette' of colours at the bottom, a box of tools represented as icons, and a central window, which in this case contains a painted mark.

The computer represents this image as a grid of tiny picture elements, or *pixels* (clearly visible when the magnifying tool is used to 'zoom in' on part of the image), and assigns a number to each pixel, denoting its colour. The numbers are stored sequentially in the computer's

Soft Still-life, George Whale, UK, 1996. Inkjet, 28 x 36cm (11 x 14.2in.). In this low-resolution image, colour dithering has been employed to achieve grainy, textured blends.

memory (RAM), such that each position in the sequence corresponds, or 'maps', to a particular pixel in the grid; this type of digital image is said to be *pixel-mapped* or (especially in the case of black and white images, where a single bit is enough to specify the colour of each pixel) bit-mapped.

Simple paint programs, many of them originating at a time when display screens were much coarser than they are now, encourage the use of flat, 'blocky' shapes in a few bold colours, which some artists have exploited to great effect and these kinds of images are often readily adaptable for screenprinting (see Chapter 6). Where colours are limited, blending from one to another is sometimes achieved by *dithering*, a process whereby coloured pixels are distributed so as to create apparently new colours in the manner of *pointilliste* painting, using optical mixing rather than intermediate colour values.

In contrast to the simplicity of applications like Windows Paint are programs like Painter, designed to reproduce, in great detail, effects associated with natural media such as watercolour, pastels, pencil and charcoal. Such 'feature-rich' applications take a little while to master, but the results can be strikingly effective.

Colour and Drawing 1: Garden Table, James Faure Walker, UK, 1998. Composite inkjet print, 81 x 56cm (32 x 22in.). Image originated with Corel Painter software.

Image processing and photo-manipulation

Applications: Adobe® Photoshop®, Jasc® Paint Shop Pro™, Synthetik Studio Artist®, Corel PhotoPaint®, HSC Live Picture®, Serif PhotoPlus.

Processes such as image sharpening, contrast adjustment and edge detection originated in the 1960s when computers were first used to enhance and analyse scientific images such as medical scans and satellite photographs. Modern applications developed for the photographic and design industries incorporate many of these processes as well as a vast range of new ones, so that all kinds of pixel-mapped images, including scanned photographs and drawings, can be edited, transformed, collaged, layered or otherwise combined.

Image-processing programs often have painting features, and vice versa. Both may be enhanced by the use of extensions, or 'plug-ins' – little additions to the program that extend its capabilities. Most scanners, for example, are supplied with a plug-in that enables scanned images to be imported directly into Photoshop, and there's a whole range of plug-in 'filters' for creating special effects, textures, and so on (e.g. Kai's Power Tools, Xaos Tools Terrazzo).

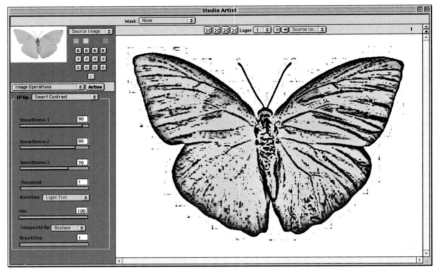

Studio Artist, an image-processing program by Synthetik, presents an interface similar to that of some music composition software: individual modules for texture synthesis, image manipulation and animation can be modified and linked together to define a sequence of processing steps.

Dog/Byte/Bark! Darren Raven, UK, 1998. Inkjet (square, various sizes). Vector drawings such as this one, made in Adobe Illustrator, can be scaled without loss of quality, facilitating printing at almost any size. Printed by Contemporary Artworks, London.

Elena, Julian Opie, UK, 1999. Billboard image, 192 x 158cm (75.6 x 62.2in.).
(© Julian Opie.) An original vector-based drawing was output to a CNC (computer
numerically controlled) cutting plotter to reconstruct the image as a set of self-
adhesive vinyl shapes, positioned and mounted on a single panel. (Vinyl cutting by
SignTec, Leighton Buzzard, UK.)

Structured drawing

Applications: Adobe Illustrator®, Macromedia® Freehand®, CorelDraw®. Geometric, or *vector-based images* are built from 'objects' – lines, curves, shapes and type, having attributes of colour, line weight, line style and fill style (pattern, gradient, etc.). The computer can represent such objects accurately and efficiently – a circle, for example, requires only four numbers to specify its horizontal and vertical position, radius and colour. This is a 'higher-level' representation than a pixel-map because, instead of being broken up into pixels, each object retains its structure and can be selected and modified at any stage in the making of a drawing.

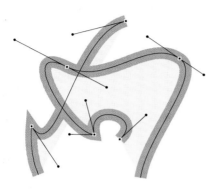

Part of a vector-based drawing, showing the 'handles' used to shift and modify shapes.

Unlike pixel-mapped images, structured drawings (illustrations, maps, logos, diagrams, etc.) are resolution-independent – they can be scaled up to almost any size without loss of quality. They can also be output to line-drawing devices (plotters), digital engraving machines, and machines that cut stencils and vinyls. Not all pictures lend themselves to geometric representation; nevertheless these kinds of digital images can greatly extend the scope of traditional print techniques, including relief and intaglio (see Chapter 5).

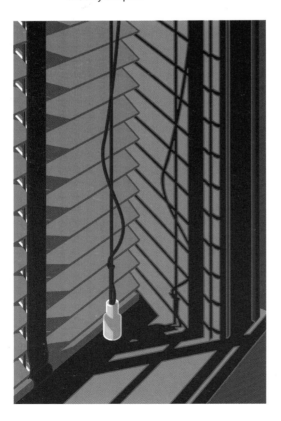

Blind, David Case, UK, 1998. Inkjet print of vector drawing (various sizes). Printed by Contemporary Artworks, London.

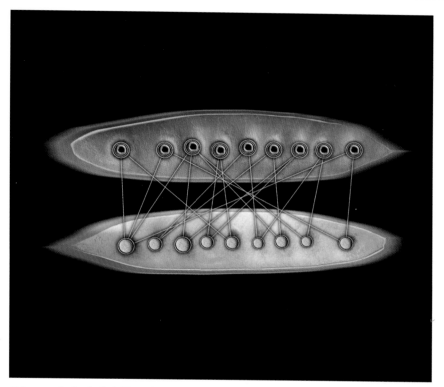

Erbsenseele (polarity), Tina Zimmermann, USA. 2000. Digital collage, 45 x 45cm (18 x 18in.). Geometric line work superimposed on recoloured scans of pea-pods, pebbles and nuts. Printed on canvas by the Digitograf® process.

Desktop publishing (DTP)

Applications: QuarkXPress™, Adobe InDesign™, Adobe PageMaker®, AppleWorks, Microsoft Publisher, Microsoft Office.

Although DTP, or page layout, applications are mainly used by graphic designers for laying out text and images and are rarely used for image origination, they can be invaluable for preparing images prior to printing. They can also be invaluable where the combination of pixel-mapped images with vector-based text and graphics of the highest quality is required.

'Virtual' modelling and rendering in three dimensions

Applications: NewTek Lightwave, AutoDesk AutoCAD®, Strata 3D™, SoftImage®, AutoDesSys FormZ, Alias/Wavefront Maya®.

By providing sets of building blocks, or 'primitives' (usually Platonic solids and a few other useful shapes) and various tools for transforming and combining them, 3D modelling applications make it possible to create

One thing or another, Tim O'Riley, UK, 2000. Durst Lambda C-type print on Fuji Crystal Archive paper, 59.5 x 74.5cm (23.4 x 29.3in.). Full-colour rendering of an original 3D model.

Banana Dance Ball Room, Vladimir Havrilla, Slovak Republic, 1998. Inkjet, from a model created with the 3D modelling/web-authoring application Caligari trueSpace.

Beneath the Rule a landscape lies, Ken Musgrave, USA, 2000. Inkjet, 107 x 160cm (42 x 63in.). (© Ken Musgrave 2000.) Image created with Pandrómeda's MojoWorld software, which enables real-time exploration of mathematically-generated planet-scapes. Printed with an Epson Stylus Pro 9500, using pigment-based, archival inks.

new forms occupying a 'virtual', three-dimensional space inside the computer. The underlying geometry comprises points, lines and triangulated surfaces, to which may be applied colours, textures or images. After interactively positioning virtual lights and cameras, the user can render the scene to produce a more or less photographic depiction of something that may never have existed. Many 3D programs have animation capabilities.

Specialist software

Sometimes, to do something unusual, it is necessary to go back to using more fundamental methods or (like the artists included in Chapter 8) to learn how to program, or to search for a program that does do what's wanted.

Specialist 2D applications include Fontographer®, for creating and modifying fonts, and Posterworks®, for making and printing billboard-size displays; 3D applications include Corel Bryce®, for synthesising mountains and landscapes, and Curious Labs Poser®, for modelling and animating human(oid) figures. There are also programs for creating textile patterns, mathematical forms, garden layouts and architectural structures, to give but a few examples.

Small programs, or utilities, abound. Adobe Streamline™ is a 2D

Coney Island Baby, Laurence Gartel, USA, 1999. Cibachrome print from photographic transparency, 25.4 x 33cm (10 x 13in.). Image created with Painter, Kai's Power Tools.

program that *vectorises* pixel-maps, that is, it turns them into line drawings. Anti-virus utilities, such as Virex (Mac) and VirusScan (PC) protect against computer viruses. For fixing disk problems and retrieving files when things go awry, Norton Utilities™ is very effective.

Colour models

Display screens are able to display a broad range, or *gamut,* of colours by mixing different amounts of red, green and blue (*RGB*) lights, the so-called additive primaries. Most software enables users to specify colours using either the RGB model or the *HSV* model (hue, saturation and value), but these often have to be converted when output, since many digital printers use the four process colours: cyan, magenta, yellow and black (*CMYK*). Conversion from RGB or HSV to CMYK can be troublesome, not least because CMYK has a smaller colour gamut – some colours are simply too intense to be printed.

WORKING WITH DIGITAL IMAGES

Table 2: Common file formats for graphics and text

FORMAT	FULL NAME	IMAGE TYPE	DESCRIPTION
3DMF or 3DM	3D Metafile	3D	Apple's cross-platform 3D file format.
BMP	Windows Bitmap	pixel-map	Standard Windows format for pixel-mapped images.
DXF	Drawing Interchange Format	3D	AutoCAD format supported by most 3D applications; a text file defining 3D model geometry.
EPS	Encapsulated PostScript	vector, page layout, pixel-map	Popular format for saving drawings and page layouts, supported by most illustration and DTP applications. Can also be used for pixel-mapped images.
FPX	FlashPix	pixel-map	Used with digital cameras, stores image at multiple resolutions, along with information about how it was created.
GIF	Graphics Interchange Format	pixel-map	Compressed format designed for electronic transmission, often used for images in web pages. Only supports 8-bit colour (256 colours or less).
HTML or HTM	Hypertext Markup Language	web page layout	HTML is a page description language (PDL) used for web pages. HTML files are best viewed in a web browser program such as Microsoft Internet Explorer, or Netscape Navigator, but can also be opened by many DTP applications.
JPEG or JPG	Joint Photographic Experts Group	pixel-map	Unlike GIF format, JPEG retains all colour information of an RGB image. Uses lossy compression method to achieve high compression ratios, but this always changes the image and is best avoided for printmaking.
PDF	Portable Document Format	page layout	Compact platform-independent document files created by the electronic publishing program Adobe Acrobat.
PICT or PCT	Apple picture format	pixel-map, vector	Intermediary format used for transferring images between Macintosh graphics and page layout applications; efficient compression of images containing solid blocks of colour or alpha channels.
PNG	Portable Network Graphics	pixel-map	An alternative to GIF for web images. Unlike GIF, preserves all colour information and alpha channels. Lossless compression.
PSD	Adobe Photoshop Document	pixel-map	Adobe Photoshop native format, able to save all components of a Photoshop image, including layers, channels and paths.
RIFF or RIF	Raster Image File Format	pixel-map	Corel Painter native format, able to save all components of a Painter image, including floating objects. Uses lossless compression.
RTF	Rich Text Format	text (and page layouts)	Formatted text, including fonts, styles, colours. File may also include images.
TIFF or TIF	Tagged Image File Format	pixel-map	Popular format for pixel-mapped images, used to exchange files between applications and computer platforms. Can accommodate different colour models, and may include alpha channels and paths. Supports lossless LZW compression.
TXT	Text	text	Plain ASCII text without additional formatting information.

Image file formats

The numerical representation of the image that is stored and continually updated in RAM whilst the image is being worked on is lost forever if the computer 'crashes', or if there's a power cut, which is why most applications have *Save* and *Save As...* commands in the *File* menu enabling the user periodically to save the data to a disk file. The *Save As...* dialog box enables selection from a list of file types, or formats.

There are many *file formats* to choose from (see Table 2), corresponding to different ways in which image data can be organised. Each application usually has its own proprietary, or 'native' format. Where work is to be printed by someone else, for example a commercial bureau, it is safest to use a standard, 'generic' format, commonly TIFF format for pixel-maps, and EPS for vector images. JPEG images can be very compact – useful where an image wouldn't otherwise fit on disk, or when it needs to be emailed to somebody – but JPEG should be avoided since it uses a *lossy* form of *compression* that damages the image, often giving rise to unsightly artifacts. TIFF files, on the other hand, does not use a *lossy* form of compression.

Although there are specialist programs for converting images from one format to another (e.g. Equilibrium DeBabelizer, HiJackPro), both Photoshop and Painter are pretty good for this: simply *File–>Open...* the image, then *File–>Save As...* remembering to select the required new format from the list in the dialog box (as shown on page 42).

Naming files

The *Save As...*dialog also contains a box in which to type a meaningful name so that the image file can be identified later. It is common practice to end the file name with a dot, followed by one of the standard extensions listed in the 'Format' column of Table 2. So, for example, an image of some biscuits might be named 'chocolate biscuits.tiff'.

When transmitting image files electronically or porting them to another computer, it is often advisable to use short file names of eight characters or less, plus a three-character extension, e.g. 'biscuits.tif'. This is because there are still some systems which have difficulty coping with long names.

Chapter 3
ALL-DIGITAL PRINTMAKING

With the hardware in place, and software installed, the artist-printmaker is ready to embark on that all-important first print. This chapter traces each step involved in the creation and processing of an original image, and its preparation and final output as a full-colour, fine art digital print.

The only requirements are access to a basic studio set-up comprising a scanner, a small- or medium-format inkjet printer, a computer running a suitable image-processing application (such as Adobe Photoshop or Paint Shop Pro) and a basic familiarity with the application (most come with online help available via the *Help* menu, and/or online or printed tutorials).

Scanning

Before making your digital print, you will first need to get an image onto your computer! There are several ways of doing this, including scanning, digital photography, Photo-CD and the Internet. In this section we will look at how to scan and print an image, using a SoHo (small office/home office) set-up typically used by many artists.

Ten steps to a perfect scan

1. *Image selection*
    The quality of a scan depends upon two factors: the quality of the original and, importantly, the type of image being scanned. Good scans can be made from most kinds of images, including photographs, photograms, printed reproductions, patterns and textures, drawings, paintings, and prints. It is best, however, to stick to continuous tone (contone) images, as postcards or pictures in magazines or books, may produce banded patterns because of their halftone dot structure.

2. *Image placement*
    Scanners do not always scan evenly over the whole area and can have 'hotspots' where the image will be captured most effectively; the best scan is usually obtained by placing the original at the centre of the scan area. Additionally, it is important to avoid placing the original at an

angle, as this would require rotating the image after it has been scanned, involving *resampling* and possible degradation of image quality.

3. **Accessing the scanner**
   The scanner can be operated either by its own software or, more commonly, via a menu in the computer's image manipulation application (Photoshop: *File–>Import–>Name of Scanner...*). This will show a dialog box which may vary from scanner to scanner. A typical example is shown at the bottom of the page.

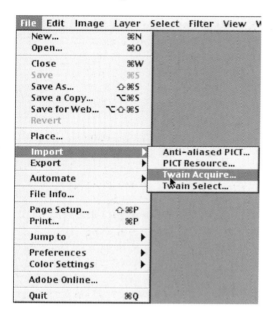

4. **Previewing the image**
   Before the original can be scanned, it should be previewed (click on the *Preview* button). This places a low-resolution version of the image in the scanner dialog box. At this stage, the preview should be checked for correct image alignment, and the original repositioned and re-previewed if necessary. The rectangular selection tool can then be used to select only the required area for scanning; scanning unwanted parts of the original takes longer, and requires more storage space.

Accessing the scanner (in Adobe Photoshop 5.5 for Mac).

Scanner dialog box for the Umax Vista scanner. The '?' button (top-right) provides help for inexperienced users.

5. *Print, transparency, or negative?*

Some scanners will offer the option to make either reflective or transmissive scans. To make transmissive scans, the scanner will require an attachment such as a transparency hood. Transmissive scans are usually of much higher quality, and possess greater density than reflective scans, and should be used when high-resolution enlargements are required. Images which have been previously screened (i.e. most printed material) pose particular problems due to their non continuous-tone nature, but many scanners now contain utilities which will attempt to remove the unwanted *banding* effects that can occur. If scanning from printed matter, search the scanner's dialog box for a *Descreen* function, and choose the option that most closely resembles the original (i.e. *Art Print, Magazine, Newspaper*). If the scanner does not possess this function, an alternative is to scan at a higher resolution while applying a *Gaussian Blur* filter.

6. *Colour mode*

The correct *colour mode* (model) should be chosen from the available options, which may include *RGB, CMYK, Grayscale* and *Lineart*. For colour originals, choose *RGB*, which is the correct mode for image manipulation applications. For continuous-tone monochrome images, or for converting a colour photograph to a black and white image, choose *Grayscale*; for making scans from logos, text and pen and ink illustrations, the *Lineart* setting is appropriate, as it will scan in solid areas of black or white only.

7. *Resolution*

Setting the correct resolution for the scan is particularly important. For a good quality print from a desktop inkjet printer, a scan resolution from 150 to 300 pixels per inch (ppi) or more at the final printout size (not the original size) will be required (see below).

8. *Scale*

How much bigger (or smaller) will the final print be when compared to the original? To obtain the correct scale for the scan, simply divide the intended length of the longest edge of the final print by the corresponding length of the original. For example, if an A4 sized print is required from an A6 original, divide the longest edge of the A4 sheet (11.9in.) by the longest edge of the A6 original (5.9in.). This gives a multiplication factor of two – an enlargement of 200% – which can then be entered in the scale box. The scale can be found by the formula:

$$\text{scale} = \frac{\text{length of longest edge of print}}{\text{length of longest edge of original}} \times 100\%$$

ALL-DIGITAL PRINTMAKING

9. *Scanner default values*

The scanner software may offer the option to modify the brightness, contrast, colour balance, tonal distribution and orientation of an image. These adjustments could be left until after the image has been scanned, since the computer's image manipulation application will have a more sophisticated set of tools for these operations.

10. *Scanning*

Once all of the options have been set correctly, the *Scan* button can be pressed. The scanner will then capture the image, the length of time taken depending on the resolution, scale and colour mode.

Saving

It is very important to save the image (Photoshop: *File–>Save As...*) as soon as it has been scanned satisfactorily, using an appropriate file format.

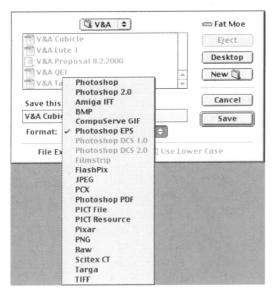

This will most commonly be the TIFF format. It is also recommended to immediately make a copy of the file, which can be used as a back-up in case of loss or damage to the scanned image (Photoshop: *File–>Save a Copy...*).

The Save As... dialog box. Entering a unique name in the text box ensures that the current version of the image is saved independently and can be retrieved (Opened) at any time. Note the list of available file formats, and the button (centre-right) for creating a new folder in which to store images.

Managing files

The number of image files will soon build up as you save more and more scans. It is important to manage these files, so that they are easily accessible and do not go astray all over your computer's hard disk. The most convenient way of doing this is to create a unique folder for each project. Choose *File–>New Folder* in the main menu. The folder can then be named, e.g. 'Scans folder'.

What? No Scanner?

Scanning may be the most convenient way of inputting existing images into the computer, but it's not the only way. A viable alternative is to use a digital camera, inputting images directly

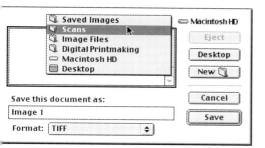

Typical folder (directory) hierarchy for an imaging project, as shown in the Photoshop *Save As...* dialog box. Here, the current image document, named 'Image 1', is to be saved in TIFF format in a folder named 'Scans' (which is inside the folder called 'Image Files').

into the computer, or to use a *Photo-CD* service, whereby pictures taken on an ordinary camera are inexpensively copied onto CD by the processing lab in several different resolutions. Pictures obtained on the Internet can also be used as source material – most are in GIF format or JPEG format, so can be opened up in programs such as Photoshop. It is important to remember, however, that images captured with a digital camera or downloaded from the Internet are unlikely to be of the quality of a scanned photographic slide or print. Also, images posted on the Internet may be subject to copyright law.

Basic image manipulation

Depending on the particular image manipulation application used, the contents and arrangement of menus, submenus and tool palettes will vary, but it is possible to do many of the post-scan corrections and basic image manipulations using any pixel-based image editing package.

Scan correction

The newly scanned image will usually need a little 'tidying up'. After saving, the first thing to check for is alignment: depending how the original was positioned on the bed of the scanner, the image may appear 'sideways-on', or even upside-down. This is easily fixed by rotating the image 90° (clockwise or counterclockwise) or 180°, for example using the *Image –> Rotate Canvas* options in Photoshop. If the image still looks 'skew', than a small arbitrary rotation can also be applied, though sometimes, for the sake of image quality, it's better just to reposition the original on the scanner and redo the scan.

Most imaging programs provide menu options for removing dust and scratch marks, for sharpening an image, or for adjusting the overall colour balance. These can be invaluable where the original is old, damaged or of poor quality but, used excessively, can sometimes have unwanted side effects. It's good policy regularly to 'zoom in' on the image for a closer look after making these kinds of changes, since some problems only become visible when an image is enlarged or printed – identified straight away, they can usually be undone. Better still, use *File–>Save As...* to save

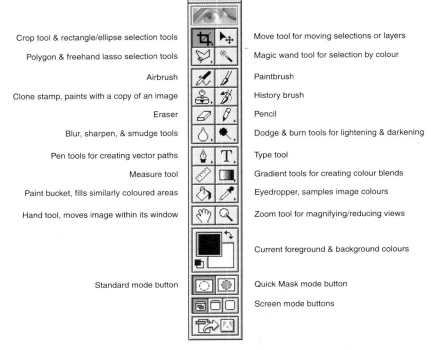

Crop tool & rectangle/ellipse selection tools	Move tool for moving selections or layers
Polygon & freehand lasso selection tools	Magic wand tool for selection by colour
Airbrush	Paintbrush
Clone stamp, paints with a copy of an image	History brush
Eraser	Pencil
Blur, sharpen, & smudge tools	Dodge & burn tools for lightening & darkening
Pen tools for creating vector paths	Type tool
Measure tool	Gradient tools for creating colour blends
Paint bucket, fills similarly coloured areas	Eyedropper, samples image colours
Hand tool, moves image within its window	Zoom tool for magnifying/reducing views
	Current foreground & background colours
Standard mode button	Quick Mask mode button
	Screen mode buttons

Photoshop floating *Tool* palette. A tools palette is a key component of most graphical applications.

successive versions of an image to the project folder on the hard drive, so that any disasters can be averted by going back to an earlier version.

Cropping

Next, the image needs to be cropped, to remove redundant areas at the edges which would otherwise take up a lot of unnecessary memory (RAM) (a 1in. border on a 4 x 5in. image, for example, would take up more space than the image itself). Another good reason for cropping is that some processes are based on average pixel colour and having a large black or white border can drastically affect the result.

Colour correction

When scanned, all the colours of a continuous-tone photograph are converted into values of red, green and blue (RGB), commonly with 256 (2^8) levels of intensity per *channel*. The 256 levels each of red, green and blue give a possible 16.7 million colours (256 x 256 x 256). In practice, you do not see quite this many colours, due to the limitations of the hardware and the human eye.

Photoshop *Variations* dialog, for applying modifications of colour and tone to an image, or selected areas. *(Image->Adjust->Variations...)*

After scanning, there may be a number of differences between the original photograph and the scan: the image on screen may appear to have lost contrast, to be too light or dark, to have lost saturation ('strength' of colour) or to have taken on an unusual colour cast. All this is normal! In attempting to resolve the thousands of colours of the continuous-tone photograph, the computer hardware and software (scanner, monitor, operating system and application) can only interpret in values of red, green and blue, often resulting in a final scan (however carefully done) with an unwanted blue or pink tint!

While many people will accept this without question, it is actually relatively easy to correct all of these unwanted effects. Menu options such as Photoshop: *Image–>Adjust–>Variations...* will enable rapid correction of any undesired deficiencies in colour, tone and saturation, by clicking on the simple on-screen icons. As a general guide, it can be expected that a scan will be less saturated, and will have insufficiently dark shadows and light highlights, when compared to the original image. Using this as a guide, it should be possible to quickly carry out any post-scan colour correction, and to develop a 'feel' for the extent of the alterations needed.

Other post-scan corrections

It may be necessary to carry out further improvements to the image after scanning. If the image has a 'noisy' or 'speckled' appearance (caused by the appearance of light pixels in dark areas or vice versa, commonly found in poor scans or scans from poor originals), apply a *Despeckle* filter (Photoshop: *Filter–>Noise–>Despeckle)* which will blur the affected areas, removing noise without losing contrast or focus in the details.

A dusty or even scratched original can be 'recovered' after scanning by applying *Filter–>Noise–>Dust & Scratches* which will remove apparent surface blemishes as if by magic! Experiment with the settings in the dialog

A freehand selection (dotted line) made with the *Lasso* tool. (Photograph by Naren Barfield.)

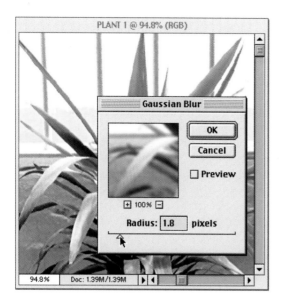

The *Gaussian Blur* filter, used to soften images, or reduce *moiré* effects arising from the scanning of printed reproductions. (*Filter->Blur-> Gaussian Blur...*)

box to avoid overdoing things, however, otherwise the image can end up appearing 'soft'.

Another filter which is often used to smooth out blemishes, particularly those caused by scanning from printed matter, is the *Gaussian Blur* filter (Photoshop: *Filter–>Blur–>Gaussian Blur...*), which can be used before sharpening to avoid a jagged appearance (staircasing).

Making selections

The actions described so far have all been global actions, affecting the entire image, but the great

Edit menu showing the *Cut, Copy, Paste,* and *Clear* commands.

strength of applications like Photoshop is their ability to work on different image areas selected by the user (local actions). There are three kinds of selection tools, which can be used in combination:

- geometric selection tools make it possible to select rectangular, elliptical or other regularly-shaped regions (the *Marquee* tool);

- with freehand tools, any shape can be selected, using a mouse or stylus to draw its outline (the *Lasso* tool);

- image-based selection tools (e.g. the Photoshop *Magic Wand* tool) make it possible to select parts of an image with similar tone, or colour.

As long as a selection is active (as indicated by an animated dotted line, or 'marching ants'), the rest of the image is effectively 'masked off', like the stencilled areas of a silkscreen: any actions will only be applied to the selected image area (or areas, in the case of a multiple selection).

Anti-aliasing (available by double-clicking any selection tool to display its *Options* palette) can be used to 'soften' the edge of a selection, without loss of detail, so that it will blend in better with the background and not appear like a cardboard cutout. It is switched either 'on' or 'off', and must be chosen *before* a selection is made. Similarly, *feathering* blurs between the selection and background over a transition defined by the user. It can be applied before a selection is made (by double-clicking a selection tool to display its *Options* palette), or afterwards (Photoshop: *Select–>Feather…*). The larger the transition used, the greater will be the loss of definition at the edge of the selection.

Cutting, copying and pasting

Many striking effects can be achieved by the simple *Edit* actions *Cut, Copy, Paste,* and *Clear,* (see menu, previous page) and transformations such as scaling and rotation, common to many applications. Each time a selection is cut or copied, the selected image area is stored in RAM ready to be pasted back into the same image, or into any other image, enabling all kinds of photomontage/collage techniques combining scanned imagery in different ways.

Resizing the image

It is possible to resize both the image (Photoshop: *Image–>Image Size…*) and the 'canvas', the (normally) invisible background on which the image sits (Photoshop: *Image–>Canvas Size…*). The image may need resizing for printing, or to fit another document; the canvas can be resized to provide more space to accommodate the expanding image as additions are made. Choosing either action will bring up a dialog box into which the user enters the desired measurements. There is a potential danger in enlarging an image: it can involve 'resampling' which can cause significant deterioration in the image quality, because the software will *interpolate* (calculate) the extra pixels needed to make up the bigger picture. If a larger print is required, it is better to return to the original and scan it at increased resolution or scale. To change the image dimensions without changing the file size (i.e. the number of pixels) deselect *Resample Image*.

Save, Save As…, or Save a Copy…?

There are times to save (*File–>Save*), i.e. every few minutes or so, or as

The Image->Image Size... dialog box in Photoshop. Used for changing image dimensions or resolution. In this example, Bicubic resampling is selected – this will give the best results in most cases.

Image Size

Pixel Dimensions: 792K

Width: 600 pixels

Height: 450 pixels

Print Size:

Width: 4 inches

Height: 3 inches

Resolution: 150 pixels/inch

OK
Cancel
Auto...

☑ Constrain Proportions
☑ Resample Image: Bicubic

long as you would be prepared to redo the work lost in a power cut! There are also times to use the other saving options. The menu command *File->Save As...* is often used to save the document (or a different version) in a different file format (as when converting from TIFF to EPS). If a copy is needed, without affecting the original file, choose *File->Save a Copy...* (or equivalent). This is the best way to save images before printing since the original is safe, and the user is additionally offered the option of flattening layers and removing unwanted *alpha channels,* which could prevent the image being imported by another application.

Preparing the image for printing

Sharpening
The last part of the correction procedure, prior to printing, is sharpening, which will rectify some of the 'softening' caused by the scanning process, and enable the optimum level of image sharpness to be obtained. This is best left to the end, once all the different elements of the image are in place. That way, the final image is sharpened as a whole, and will appear more convincing than a combination of parts which have been individually sharpened by different amounts.

A quick glance at Photoshop sharpening options reveals that there are four choices: *Sharpen, Sharpen Edges, Sharpen More,* and the curiously named *Unsharp Mask* (a term borrowed – like much in digital imaging – from photography). Choose *Filter->Sharpen->Unsharp Mask...*

The dialog box will have fields for the *Amount, Radius* and *Threshold* of the filter. Try an *Amount* of between 150 and 200%, a *Radius* of 1 to 2 pixels, and a *Threshold* of up to 20. Experiment with these settings to see which gives the best results, taking care not to use too high a radius, which would result in 'ghosting' – the appearance of a conspicuous halo around

ALL-DIGITAL PRINTMAKING

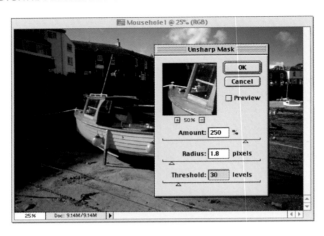

Using *Unsharp Mask* is a key part of the correction process. (*Filter–>Sharpen–> Unsharp Mask...*)

the edges of objects. This is particularly important on lower-resolution images (up to about 200 ppi); an increased *Radius* can be used in conjunction with a higher resolution. This extremely useful filter works by increasing the contrast between a pixel and its near neighbours. *Amount* determines by how much the contrast is increased. *Radius* will set the range (how many neighbouring pixels are sampled), and *Threshold* will specify by how much a pixel must differ tonally from its neighbours before it is sharpened.

The result? An image which is sharper in the detailed areas, but unchanged in flatter or undetailed areas. This is because there is greater tonal difference in areas of detail, and little or no difference in areas of flat colour. Hence a much sharper final image, rather like re-focussing a camera, but without the introduction of artifacts (stray or unwanted pixels) that a uniform sharpening might bring.

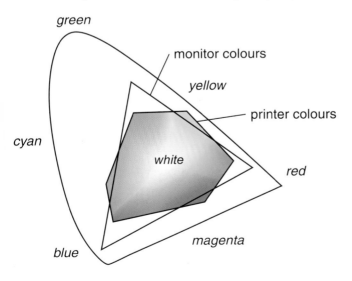

C.I.E. (*Commission Internationale de l'Eclairage*) chromaticity diagram. All visible pure colours lie on the border of the horseshoe shape; points inside represent partially saturated colours. The two inner shapes, representing the colour ranges (gamuts) of a typical RGB monitor, and of a CMYK printer, show that many (additive) colours displayable on a computer screen cannot be reproduced by (subtractive) colour printing.

Printing

Assuming, of course, that the printer is connected and switched on, and that the printer driver software has been correctly installed on the computer, only three steps remain. First, the paper size and orientation must be set in the Page Setup dialog *(File->Page Setup...)*. Then, in the Print dialog box *(File->Print...)*, the required print settings are selected (for guidance on print settings, consult the printer manual or online help). The final step is to press the *Print* button.

With the correct settings, most modern desktop printers will do a reasonable job of converting the (additive) RGB image colours to printed colours. However, the match will rarely be exact, since the majority of

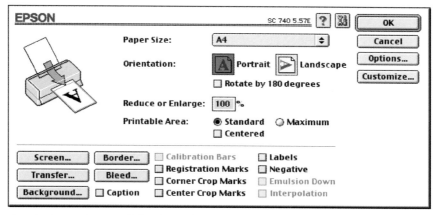

A typical *Page Setup...* dialog box, where paper size and image orientation must be set before printing.

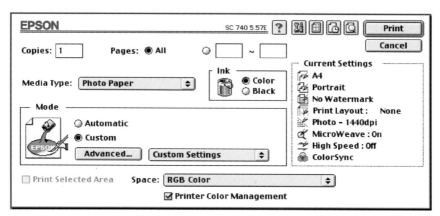

A *Print...* dialog box. The final stage in outputting a print is to press the *Print* button, having first selected the type of media being used (e.g photo paper, clear film), and other printer settings. Some experimentation is usually needed to find the best settings. Here, *Space* is set to RGB and *Printer Color Management* is checked (on) – this will usually give good results when printing RGB images.

printers use subtractive colours - usually CMYK, or an augmented six-colour set with light cyan and light magenta inks. Certain colours, particularly vivid oranges, bright greens and saturated violets are especially badly affected, since the printing inks are unable to represent the full RGB range, or gamut. Results may also be affected by the choice of substrate.

The setting up of a system to ensure accurate and predictable colour printing is an important aspect of colour management, a topic which will be returned to in the next chapter.

Materials for inkjet printmaking

If small-format inkjet printers generally cost less than lasers, they can be more expensive to run, because of the cost of consumables. Matt, satin and glossy inkjet papers are available in different weights, in sheet or roll form; there are also various types of specially coated films and plastics. For optimum quality and permanence, manufacturers recommend particular combinations of inks and substrates (usually their own) and prints made on ordinary photocopier paper are rarely satisfactory. Printers having separate tanks or cartridges for each colour (e.g. Canon printers) may be more economical than those with combined colour cartridges. Refill kits are available for some types of cartridges.

Lyson (UK) specialise in the manufacture of *archival* quality inks and papers (including acid-free fine art papers) suitable for most types of inkjet printer. Details can be found on the company's website (see Supplies and Services) along with the results of independent permanency tests conducted on different ink/substrate combinations. Most manufacturers of inkjet printers also produce a range of longer-lasting inks and papers, as do some traditional fine art paper manufacturers. As with traditional prints, the quality of mounting/framing will have an impact on the longevity of digital prints, and so will the environmental conditions in which they are stored or displayed.

Reminder

Remember, before doing anything creative with images, it is important to get the best results from scans. If the input is of poor quality, it is difficult to rectify at a later stage. As a quick reminder, the procedure from scan to print can be summarised as:

Scan > Save > Rotate/Crop > Colour/Tonal Corrections > Remove Noise/Dust/Scratches > Gaussian Blur > Image Editing/Manipulation > Unsharp Mask > Page Setup > Print

Remembering to save versions of the file at several stages along the way!

Chapter 4
MORE ADVANCED TECHNIQUES

Once the practice of scanning, correcting, making selections, manipulating and printing digital images has become familiar, it will be possible to move on to more advanced techniques that will enable ideas to develop further, while possessing many parallels to the processes and ways of thinking of traditional printmaking.

Channels

One of the most useful pieces of knowledge about digital imaging for the artist-printmaker to possess is an awareness of *channels*. Pixel-mapped images are comprised of channels. A channel is the closest analogy to the individual screen or plate in printmaking. In an RGB file, there is a channel for each colour, red, green and blue, so it's a three-channel image. A CMYK file has four channels. Each channel is like the cyan, magenta, yellow or black plate used in process printing. Easy! *Grayscale* images, containing information about a single colour, have one channel, as do the *Bitmap, Duotone* and *Indexed Color* modes. To see the channels in a Photoshop file, choose *Window–>Show Channels*, and the *Channels* palette will appear. This is one of several floating palettes which enable the application's functions to be kept close at hand.

Channels really come into their own when a selection needs to be saved for using or editing later on, or for working with colours for printing outside the process-colour CMYK model, such as specially-mixed (spot) colours – effectively, most of the inks used in traditional printmaking.

The *Channels* palette in Photoshop, showing a selection saved as a mask in an alpha channel.

A selection border (made in the normal way using any of the selection tools) can be stored with the image file as a mask (described below) using extra channels called *alpha channels*. In Photoshop, choosing *Select–>Save Selection...* or (from the pop-out submenu in the *Channels* palette) *New Channel...* will convert the selection to a mask, and save it in an alpha channel. (This can also be done by clicking the icon at the bottom of the palette.) The main advantage of this is that the mask is stored, making it

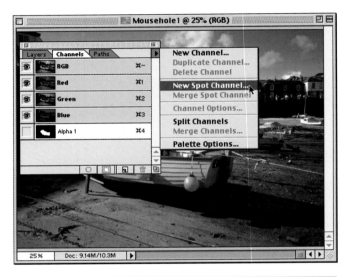

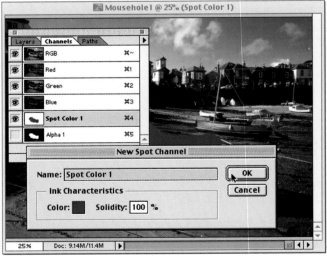

Creating a *New Spot Channel*. Spot channels can be used to preview images in the ink colours which will be used for printing by traditional methods.

permanent for future use, and can be edited at any time. Several such alpha channels can be saved with an image, meaning that the artist can return to any of the masking options they have created. The selections will appear as greyscale thumbnail images in the *Channels* palette. Edited masks can then be re-loaded as selections for use on the image.

Directly analogous to the printmaker's practice – printing each screen or plate in a distinct, individually-mixed ink which builds up the image in several discrete layers – the ability to create *spot channels* is one of the most useful features in digital imaging, since it enables a colour to be output to a single positive, instead of being separated into cyan, magenta, yellow and black. Use Photoshop to create special colours by choosing *New Spot Channel…* from the pop-out submenu in the *Channels* palette. Then click on the *Color* chip in the dialog box, and choose the desired colour from any of the *Custom Colors*, or from the *Color Picker*. This feature enables the artist to choose a colour on-screen to match the (litho, screen, etching) inks available in the print studio. Spot channels can also be created by converting an alpha channel (by double-clicking the alpha channel name in the *Channels* palette), so a masked area of the image can be turned into a plate for printing. The possibilities are endless!

Masking

In addition to using selections, masking is another way of isolating parts of the image. Masks are created by converting a selection (Photoshop: *Select–>Save Selection…* or selecting *New Channel…* from the *Channels* palette). Whereas selections are characterised by an outline – an animated border of 'marching ants' – a mask works by covering parts of the image so that they are protected from changes. The image can then be edited or manipulated (e.g. painted over) without the masked area being affected. The mask itself can also be edited using any of the painting tools in the *Tool* palette. Additionally, temporary masks can be created (using the *Quick Mask* edit mode), and individual layers in an image can be masked using layer masks.

Using the Quick Mask mode

The easiest way to mask part of an image is to use the Photoshop *Quick Mask* editing mode via the *Tool* palette. The *Quick Mask* mode enables the artist to use any of the painting tools (airbrush, paintbrush, pencil) to paint on a mask, without needing to use the *Channels* palette. This enables irregular, gestural, and non-contiguous masks to be created, by painting over the image, instead of drawing around it. This is great for masking difficult irregular areas, such as individual strands of hair (where the colour may be similar to the background, and drawing an outline would be

MORE ADVANCED TECHNIQUES

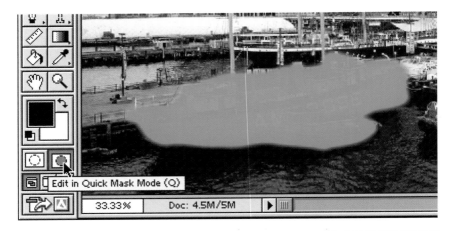

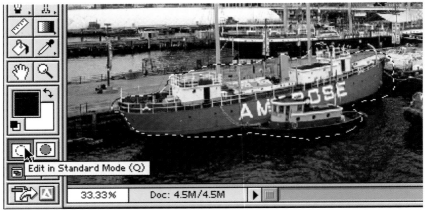

Using *Quick Mask* editing mode to paint a mask, which is then converted to a selection border by returning to Standard mode.

impossible) or simply for separating parts of an image by 'scribbling' over them.

To work with the *Quick Mask* mode, first reset the *Color Picker* in the Photoshop palette to the default black and white. This is important because the mask depends upon the opacity with which it is applied – anything less than 100% opacity will give a partial mask, although this can be chosen for intentional effect. Next, choose a painting tool from the palette, and double-click the tool to bring up its options. Choose an appropriate size and opacity (again, the opacity will affect the strength and effectiveness of the mask). A good tip is to use full opacity over the main part of the area to be masked, and a reduced opacity around the edges. This will give a softer edge to the mask so that it doesn't look obvious. Finally, click on the *Quick Mask* mode icon in the *Tool* palette, and paint away!

The painted areas will become covered in a graffiti-like layer of 'paint'. Don't worry – it hasn't altered the image; the painted area only indicates where the mask is. If the colour which indicates the mask is too similar to the colour of the image, choose a different colour by double-clicking the *Quick Mask* mode icon, and then choosing the *Color Picker* in the dialog box. Incidentally, the opacity can be altered in this box, but it will only affect the *Quick Mask* preview. After painting over the the desired areas, click on the *Standard* mode icon in the *Tool* palette. The image will return to 'normal' with a selection border now indicating the protected area. Editing now carried out will not affect the masked area.

Layering

The image layering features offered by packages such as Photoshop and Illustrator could almost have been designed with printmakers in mind, since they make it possible to build up an image in successive, independent *layers*, much as familiar printmaking processes enable an artist to apply any number of impressions, in register, onto a single sheet of paper.

Working with layers

It's easiest to think of layers like 'acetates', each containing part of the information which, when combined with other layers, makes up the whole image. The image can be manipulated as a whole (i.e. all layers), or one or more layers can be isolated and edited separately, so that only part of the image is affected. Additionally, the order of layers can be changed so that the image 'stacks' differently. Unlike acetate, layers are easily rescaled and edited. They are invaluable for trying out different combinations of elements, or for isolating parts of an image to be printed separately.

When an image is first created (either by creating a 'drawing' on the computer, or by acquiring an image through scanning or other means), it exists on a single plane, to which more layers can be added. Adding layers is very straightforward, and can be done in a number of ways:

Creating a new layer via the menu

Using Photoshop (which allows up to 100 layers to be created in a single file) as an example, create a new layer by going to the pull-down menu bar and selecting *Layer–>New–>Layer…* In the dialog box which appears, give the layer a name (e.g. 'biscuits') and click on *OK*. The new layer is now ready to be worked on.

Creating a new layer via the Layers palette

An alternative way of creating a new layer is via the *Layers* palette (*Window–>Show Layers*). Pressing down on the small arrow at the top right corner of the palette will activate a pop-out submenu which offers *New Layer...* Enter information in the dialog. A new layer can also be created simply by mouse-clicking the small *New Layer* icon at the bottom of the *Layers Palette.* This will create a layer without calling up the dialog box, unless *Option-click* (Mac) or *Alt-click* (PC) is used.

New layer using the Copy and Paste commands

Make a selection in the image using any of the selection tools. Go to the pull-down menu item: *Edit–>Copy.* The selection will now be temporarily stored in the clipboard, waiting to be pasted into this, or a different, file. Move the selection to the desired position, and using the pull-down menu select *Edit–>Paste.* This will place the selection where required, but it will also create a new layer for this pasted selection to 'live' on (this will be seen in the *Layers* palette). This is extremely useful as it enables the selection to be repositioned, distorted, or manipulated in some other way, without affecting the original background image. This technique can also be used to paste a selection from one image to another: simply use the *Edit–>Copy* command to make a selection, open another image file (*File–>Open...*) and select *Edit–>Paste* as above. The selection will now be pasted as a new layer into the newly-opened image file.

Parts of the original image can also be copied onto other layers, or separated from the original. Use Photoshop: *Layer–>New–>Layer via Copy* or *Layer–>New–>Layer via Cut* to achieve this.

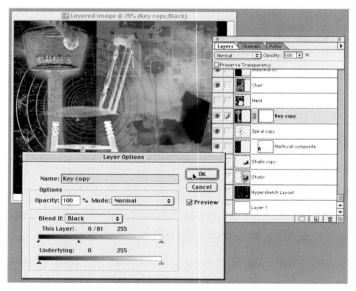

The *Layer->Layer Options...* dialog box can be used to alter the blending between layers.

Additional layers features

Many additional features are available both through the *Layers* palette and the *Layer* menu in Photoshop. Explore these for ways of affecting the opacity and transparency, and blending between layers, using the sliders in the *Layer Options* dialog (via the *Layer* palette submenu; by double-clicking the layer in the *Layers* palette, or via *Layer–>Layer Options...* in the menu.) This enables smoother and more convincing combining of different layers, and for parts of one layer to emerge 'through' another.

Normal editing (scaling, perspective, distort, etc.) can be applied to individual layers, as can a number of special effects (Photoshop: *Layer–>Effects*) which include such useful features as drop shadows and embossing, which will exclusively affect the active layer.

When combined with masking, individual layers can be edited to create 'knockouts' or graduated transparencies where one layer appears to fade into the layer(s) underneath. A layer mask covers parts or all of a layer, rendering it transparent, without actually altering the image on that layer. Choose Photoshop: *Layer–>Add Layer Mask–>Reveal All* for a layer-specific mask that is created by any of the painting tools; or *Layer–>Add Layer Mask–>Hide All* to create a mask that covers the layer, and is subtracted from to reveal parts of the image. Adding a layer mask creates an alpha channel in the *Layers* palette, linked to the layer it affects, and which is saved with the file. It is important to remember that layered images can only be saved in the native Photoshop file format (PSD) and may need flattening (Photoshop: *Layer–>Flatten Image*) before printing or placing in another application.

A word about colour management

Colour management – the attempt to control the way in which colour is represented digitally and transferred between applications, devices, platforms and printers – is just about the most difficult thing there is to learn in digital imaging. There are books and careers devoted to this extremely complex subject, and we recommend looking into it when you feel confident (and when your green images print out pink).

As a digital file makes its journey from original image to final inkjet (or alternative) print, it passes via the scanner, computer hardware and operating system, monitor, imaging application, and colour printer, all of which may use different, if not incompatible, colour ranges (gamuts). As if this wasn't bad enough, taking the digital file from one computer to another, or across platform from Mac to PC, or to a bureau for output, only exacerbates the problem – and that is without trying to get the colour in a print to match the image on the monitor! In the long run, the best solution to the situation is to create a 'closed system' where all equipment is calibrated to work well together, but this requires both expertise and patience.

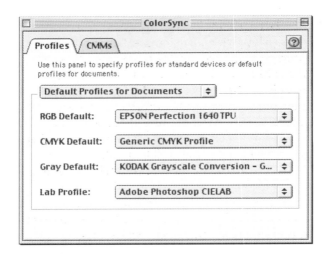

Control panel for Apple ColorSync system- wide colour management; enables calibration of the system for optimal colour reproduction.

For the moment, here are a few things worth knowing. To attempt to address the problems of colour incompatibility between devices, digital 'boffins' have devised Colour Management Systems, (or CMSs) which understand the different colour capabilities, or ICC (International Color Consortium) *profiles*, of given equipment. These systems then attempt to 'map' the colour from one profile to another as accurately as possible, replacing any out-of-gamut colours with near approximations. This was first brought in at an operating system level with Apple ColorSync® (for the Mac platform), followed later with ICM for Windows 95 (PC). When adding a new piece of equipment to a set-up (such as a new scanner), the CD which contains the software for the device will install its ICC profile into the computer's operating system, enabling it to be recognised and understood by other devices and applications. If all such profiles are correctly installed, reasonable colour conversion between devices and applications can be expected (in theory at least).

In practice, the only thing required is to ensure that the computer's Colour Management System (ColorSync or ICM) is switched on and set up correctly for any connected devices, that the monitor is calibrated (set up to display colours correctly – usually via a control panel in the computer operating system or via the application), and that the application uses the correct device profiles (such as Photoshop: *File–>Color Settings–>Profile Setup…*).

The website of Cone Editions Press (see Supplies and Services) offers much useful information on colour management for desktop inkjet printing and is a recommended first step on the long journey to perfect colour. For a comprehensive treatment of colour management, Martin Evening's *Adobe Photoshop for Photographers* (Focal Press) is also highly recommended.

Outputting positives for printmaking

There are many possible ways of applying digital images to traditional print matrices, some of which are explored in Chapters 5 and 6. One popular method is to make one or more halftoned positives from the image, transferring them to plates or screens by standard photo-based means. Traditionally-printed digital images will normally be of lower resolution than their all-digital counterparts, because of the technical limitations of the traditional print matrices and the difficulties of printing fine work by hand. It is advisable to plan ahead and to decide which print process(es) will be used, in advance of doing the first scan. This is because the output requirements for each process are different, and the image needs to be optimised for whichever one is used – and for whether the positive is to be made professionally at a bureau, or using basic equipment in a studio set-up. Both the image quality (density, sharpness and definition), and of course the expense, will be far greater when obtaining film output from high-end devices such as imagesetters (at bureaux), than when using commonly available laser or inkjet printers to produce paper or acetate positives.

MORE ADVANCED TECHNIQUES

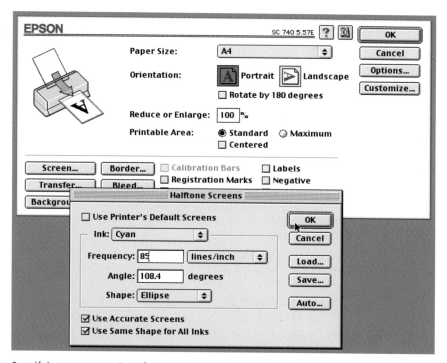

Specifying screen settings for outputting (simulated) halftones from Photoshop (in the *File–>Page Setup...–>Screen...* dialog box).

Halftones or dithers?

When creating positives for printmaking, the pixel-mapped image does not emerge from the printer still comprised of pixels. It is converted by the software into patterns of dots, either clustered or distributed, known as *simulated halftones* or *dither patterns,* respectively. Both enable the printing of photographic-type images in a range of apparent tones.

Dithering, with its tiny, apparently randomised dots and fine detail can be useful for generating different textures, and for avoiding the problems of *moiré* patterning when overprinting conventional halftones. Some output devices (particularly inkjet printers) will automatically output images using dithering. Alternatively, dithering can be imposed on the image itself (Photoshop: *Image–>Mode–>Grayscale* then: *Image–>Mode–>Bitmap…* then select *Diffusion Dither*. Try this method several times, entering different values in the *Resolution* field until the desired effect is achieved.) In every case, care must be taken that the diffused dots are not so small that they will be unable to transfer to plate or screen or, if having done so, they are too fine to print on conventional presses.

Simulated halftones have largely replaced photographically-produced halftones as a means of producing plates and screens for commercial printing. This process produces the familiar halftoned four-colour images seen on billboards, in newspapers and magazines, and on packets of breakfast cereal. Their use for the artist-printmaker lies in their proven reliability as a method, their flexibility, and their (relatively) straightforward translation into the print processes.

Calculating a halftone screen

A halftone screen is comprised of information about the shape, size and orientation of the dots, and their frequency (how many dots there are in a given measurement, usually measured in lines per inch, or *lpi*). This can be left to the application's default setting, but a little understanding of screen frequency (to give it its proper name) is invaluable for getting the most out of the digital-to-traditional print conversion.

Detail versus tone

Screen frequency will affect the detail in a print. Quite simply, a higher frequency will mean more dots packed into a given space, and so more detail. So, go for maximum frequency? Not quite. Due to the way in which digital halftones are made, there is an inescapable trade-off between detail and the number of grey levels, or tones, that can be reproduced. In other words, more detail equals less tones; and *vice versa*. Without going to great lengths to explain how or why this trade-off happens (there are several books on the subject, some of them readable), there is a short formula which will enable the user to work out the number of tones that will be created by a printer of given resolution when outputting digital halftones. The formula is:

$$\text{number of grey levels (tones)} = \left(\frac{\text{maximum printer resolution (dpi)}}{\text{halftone screen frequency (lpi)}} \right)^{2} + 1$$

which is read as 'maximum printer resolution divided by halftone screen frequency all squared plus one'. Thus, for a 600 dpi laser printer, using a halftone screen of 75 lines per inch will result in a halftoned image containing $(600 \div 75)^{2} + 1 = 65$ tones, or levels of grey.

For the same printer, a higher screen ruling (more detail) would result in fewer tones; a lower ruling would increase the tonal range. Think of it like a see-saw. It is therefore important, given any output device, to know which screen ruling is most appropriate for creating the desired tonal range. As an example, a range of screen rulings and the resulting tonal range for a 600 dpi and 1200 dpi laser printer, and a 2400 dpi imagesetter, is given below.

Table 3: Relationship between detail and tones in digital halftoning			
	600 dpi laser printer	1200 dpi laser printer	2400 dpi imagesetter
Number of tones at 60 lpi	101	401	1601
Number of tones at 85 lpi	51	199	798
Number of tones at 100 lpi	37	145	577
Number of tones at 150 lpi	17	65	257

As table 3 shows, detail and tone are inversely related. Additionally, the higher the maximum resolution of the output device, the greater the range of tones at a given screen ruling. As a guide, anything less than seventeen tones will begin to produce noticeable posterisation effects and, unless specifically wanted, is not recommended.

Screen rulings and traditional printmaking
The fun doesn't end there! Each of the main print processes has an optimum range of screen rulings (see table 4), based on the amount of halftone information the plate or screen can be expected to hold, and how much information can be adequately reproduced using hand-printing.

Emulsion up or down?
When printing out a positive for transfer to one of the traditional print processes, it is important which side of the film or acetate the emulsion

(the image-bearing surface) is. This is because it will affect whether or not the image is right-reading when printed (see table 4).

Table 4: Screen rulings and emulsions			
	Screen frequency (lpi)	Scan resolution (ppi)	Emulsion up or down
Etching	up to 100	up to 200	up
Offset lithography	up to 85	up to 170	down
Screenprinting	up to 65	up to 130	up

Screen rulings and image resolution

Wait, there's more! The halftone dots are there to try and capture information from the pixel-mapped image, and render it with as much detail and accuracy as is possible. If the image is particularly low-resolution, information will be lost and it will not look very good. Be careful, however, at the other end of the scale: too much image resolution, and the halftone dots won't be able to do the image justice. Again, there is a formula for calculating the relationship. It is:

$$\text{halftone (lpi)} \quad = \quad \frac{\text{image resolution (dpi)}}{2}$$

It's that simple, but remember what this means: before scanning an image, it is helpful to know what the screen ruling will be when the image is printed.

Reminder

The whole process of scanning and outputting a pixel-mapped image for traditional printmaking can be summed up as:

What is the optimum screen ruling of the chosen print process? > Double it to obtain the scan resolution > What output device will be used for generating positives? > What tonal range will this give? > Make any adjustments as necessary

To do all of this, you will need to be able to set the screen ruling manually. Do this in Photoshop, *File–>Page Setup…* and then in the Photoshop settings, click on *Screen…* Turn off *Use Printer's Default Screen*, and enter a value for the halftone screen frequency. A CMYK image will require four frequencies (one for each colour); a grayscale image will require only one. While here, enter the desired halftone dot shape, and the screen angle.

Obtaining positives from bureaux

Start by deciding how big the finished print is to be, based on the size (and cost) of the available plates or blocks and (where appropriate) the size of negatives/positives that can be produced, then set up the dimensions of the source digital image(s) accordingly. This will avoid problems of scaling, and will help in estimating the resolution of any scans that need to be done. Remember also that not all bureaux can produce film bigger than A3 and, even if they can, the cost can be prohibitive.

To avoid wastage, do test exposures when using new or unfamiliar photo-based materials. When using layered images for multi-impression prints, registration can be facilitated by creating an additional, base layer with registration marks placed on it. This can be printed out with each layer, ensuring identical positioning on each.

PostScript – outputting vector images

PostScript® is a page description language (PDL) developed by Adobe to describe the positions, sizes, colours, and other attributes of type and graphics arranged on a page. PostScript is used by most drawing programs and shares the big advantage of all vector-based descriptions, that the quality of output is entirely dependent on the resolution of the output device, in other words it is resolution-independent – even low-resolution output seen on a screen or an inexpensive printer provides a good guide to how the page will appear when output to another device, such as an imagesetter.

PostScript printers (the more expensive lasers) are recommended for vector-based drawings and page layouts, as they contain RAM and processing power which enables them to interpret and print PostScript files sent from the computer. For non-PostScript printers (most inkjets), special software is available to improve the printing of PostScript fonts or graphics – for example Adobe Type Manager® (for fonts), and Birmy PowerRIP (for graphics), are both compatible with PCs and Macs.

Archives and edition records

Archiving refers to the storage of proofs, print files (on CD), and other information necessary to complete an edition or replace a print at a later date. To some extent, archiving is an act of faith, since it is based on the (dubious) assumption that the materials and equipment will not, in the meantime, become obsolete! Doubts have also been expressed about the relevance of traditional editioning procedures to digital printmaking. Nevertheless, accurate records of unusual materials and processes will always be of value, not least to future conservators and restorers. (Guidance on these matters is available from organisations such as the American Print Alliance – see Other Information Sources, page 124.)

Untitled, Naren Barfield, UK, 2000. Screenprint, 50 x 60cm (19.7 x 23.6in.). Developed as a multi-layer Photoshop image, and saved in EPS format for placement in QuarkXPress. The QuarkXPress document was sent to a bureau to be imageset to film (screen ruling 65 lpi), and the image transferred to a fine mesh screen coated with sensitized photo-stencil. Constituent layers are shown in various combinations.

Three layers, comprising the white base-layer, scans of mathematical drawings (inverted to make them white on black), and a photograph (scanned at 150 ppi) with light areas rendered transparent using *Layer Options.*

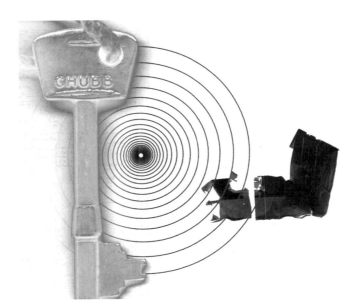

The spiral is an imported vector drawing; the image of the key (scanned directly from the object) uses a graduated layer mask for blending.

The inverted, transparent chair image has further layers of
mathematical notation superimposed.

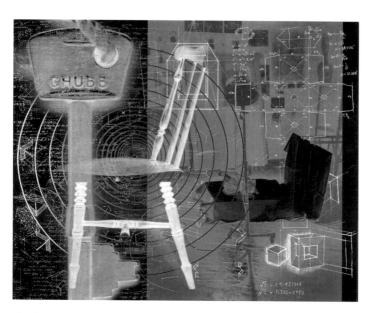

The final image - all layers have been combined, and white airbrush applied.

Chapter 5

INTEGRATION WITH RELIEF, INTAGLIO AND COLLOTYPE

As it becomes increasingly difficult to distinguish digital prints from familiar kinds of prints, a temptation is to scrap the old presses and 'go digital'. But there are those who, whilst committed to exploring the computer's capabilities, still enjoy working with physical materials, and recognise that there are issues to do with surface quality and fineness of control which all-digital printmaking hasn't yet resolved. Many artists have devised ways of integrating digital imaging with traditional print media: so-called 'hybrid', or 'tradigital' techniques. This chapter will look at some of the ways in which computers can be used in the making of intaglio, relief and collotype prints.

Vector-based photo-etching

The linear, hard-edged character of structured drawings makes them readily adaptable for intaglio work. As will be seen later in this chapter, digital engraving machines can be used to cut a drawing directly into the surface of a plate or block, but for those lacking access to such technology, high quality results can be achieved by photo-chemical means, using a conventional UV exposure unit to transfer a photo-positive of the vector image to a sensitised surface. The steps are as follows:

1. Preparation

In the drawing program, select a standard paper size a few centimetres wider and higher than the required image size, to make sure that the edges of the image aren't 'clipped' during output. Use the program's ruler guides to position registration marks at the corners of the image area; crosshairs can be made from pairs of line segments around 0.5 pt in weight.

2. Creating the drawing

A few points are worth bearing in mind: fine lines and textures may appear deceptively thick on screen, so zoom in periodically to check relative line weights; broader lines and shapes, unless broken up into smaller elements, may not hold ink evenly when the etching plate is finally inked up and may

Chart 1: some routes from the pixel-mapped image to the print matrix.

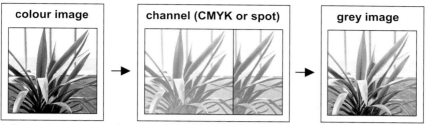

1. From colour to greyscale
Make a copy of the colour image, then convert the copy to greyscale (*Image->Mode->Grayscale*). Alternatively, convert CMYK (or spot colour) channels to greyscale by copying each one individually and pasting it into a new image.

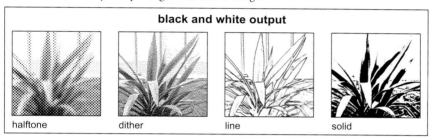

2. Greyscale to black and white
A greyscale image is automatically converted to black and white when output to a laser or inkjet printer, or to an imagesetter. The particular kind of halftoning or dithering used will depend on the settings in the *Print* dialog box. It is also possible to convert to black and white within the application, before printing, using *Image->Mode->Bitmap…*, or *Image->Adjust->Threshold…*, or a special filter such as *Mezzotint* or *Graphic Pen* in Photoshop.

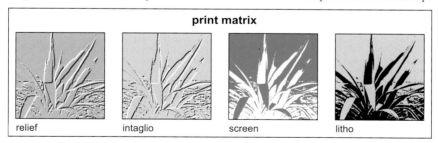

3. Making the matrix
Film or paper prints produced by laser or inkjet printers, or by an imagesetter, can be used as positives for photo-screenprinting, photo-litho, or photo-etching. If the image is inverted before printing (*Image->Adjust->Invert*), the output can be used as a negative, e.g. for collotype.

Special materials for laser printing include toner transfer paper, used for transferring images directly to etching plates. There are also synthetic litho plates, which are hand-fed through the printer. They require minimal processing, and provide a quick and inexpensive way of turning digital images into lithographs (see Supplies and Services).

Another interesting option is laser engraving - a greyscale or black and white image file can be sent to a manufacturer for cutting directly into a wood or plastic relief block of almost any size. This technique, like some of the others mentioned here, can also be used with vector-based images.

Jacket and Book, from the series *My Father's Coat,* Paul Coldwell, UK, 1996. Etching and aquatint, 40 x 28cm (15.7 x 11in.). Layered drawing made in Adobe Illustrator and transferred to zinc photo-etching plate via imageset film positive. Coldwell often prefers a mouse to a stylus for interactive drawing, and uses multiple layers as a way of managing complexity. He observed that 'When using a drawing program... choices have to be made as to whether the line is to be broken, continuous, soft-edged, hard-edged, square or round-ended.'

Etchings from *My Father's Coat* contain line motifs and patterns vectorised from scanned images using Adobe Streamline. Inkjet proofing was employed throughout.

have to be reworked later (see step 5). Remember to save (versions of) the evolving drawing regularly, so that it is always possible to backtrack.

3. Making the positive

A laser or inkjet print, in black ink on standard 80 gsm white paper, can make an excellent photo-positive, but requires an exposure several times longer than film. Prints on clear or matt acetate may have sufficient density, given the right combination of toner/ink and acetate. Alternatively, a process camera can be used to copy a paper positive to film. For images containing fine detail, or where precise registration of multiple impressions is required, imagesetting is the best option. An *imagesetter* is a high-resolution device that transfers digital images directly to film. Many digital output bureaux have them, and can process a file within 24 hours. (See Chapter 7: *Preparing Work for Professional Output*.) Film positives for etching, whether produced by an imagesetter or by some other method, should always be emulsion up; in other words, when looking at the image right-way-round, the emulsion (matt) side should be uppermost.

4. Exposure

The positive is placed face down on a pre-sensitised photo-etching plate to give the customary inverted image. Since the emulsion side (or printed side, in the case of a paper positive) is in direct contact with the plate, the risk of 'undercutting' of light during exposure is minimised, ensuring maximum crispness of lines and edges. With the positive taped in position, the plate is exposed. Exposure times will vary depending on the plate, exposure unit and positive being used: experiment to establish the optimum set-up for a particular studio.

5. Working the plate

Once the plate has been developed, all of the traditional techniques of etching can be applied. Computer-made forms can be augmented with the autographic qualities of hand-drawn marks, or broad lines and shapes given additional weight and density by aquatinting. Registration marks are blocked out before biting.

6. Printing

Inking and printing can be done conventionally, or can be combined with digitally printed work: some inkjet inks are sufficiently water-resistant that when printed onto suitable paper, they can be judiciously dampened to receive an etching – a potential alternative to traditional hand colouring.

INTEGRATION WITH RELIEF, INTAGLIO, AND COLLOTYPE

Pyramid in Black and White Number One, Isaac Victor Kerlow, USA, 1985. Etching, 51 x 40cm (20 x 15.7in.). Drawings made directly on the plate were combined with rendered 3D computer models transferred photographically. Kerlow's *Seven Pyramids in Black and White* derive from sketches made in Mayan and Mixtec sites in Mexico.

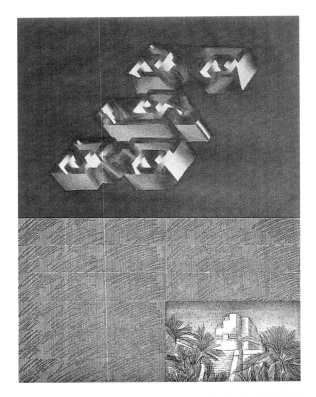

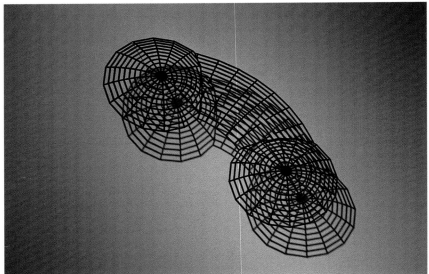

Dard, Max Davison, UK, 1998. Etched metal. 40 x 50cm (15.7 x 19.7in.). A line plot of a wire-frame 3D model was screenprinted onto sheet metal, which was subsequently etched.

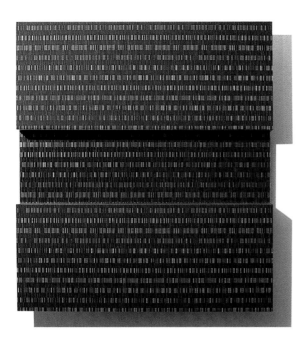

Inset-Scan Me, Friedhard Kiekeben, Germany, 1997. Zinc plate and etchings, 78 x 64 x 7cm (30.7 x 25.2 x 2.8in.). Pixel-maps were etched into a zinc plate, which was then folded and combined with two etchings taken from the plate.

Etchings from pixel-maps

To use continuous-tone images in etching, they must first be broken down into elements of a single colour, for example by halftoning. With image processing applications, it is possible to simulate 'classical', photographic halftones or, alternatively, to employ digital halftoning techniques such as dithering, where dots vary in distribution rather than size.

Tapestry II, Charlotte Hodes, UK, 1996. Colour etching and aquatint, 34 x 29cm (13.4 x 11.4in.). A scanned image of a figure was halftoned, imported into Illustrator, and overlaid on a pattern of geometric ellipses. The combined layers were imageset to create a single film positive (emulsion-side up), which was exposed onto a pre-coated copper photo-etching plate. Aquatint was applied to the figure, and the pattern deeply etched to give a white emboss. The figure was inked separately, and the whole plate then surface-rolled.

INTEGRATION WITH RELIEF, INTAGLIO, AND COLLOTYPE

Tapestry III, Charlotte Hodes, UK, 1996. Colour etching, 34 x 29cm (13.4 x 11.4in.). Layered pixel-map transferred to a single plate, inked *á la poupee*, and printed intaglio.

Charlotte Hodes has achieved some remarkable textural effects incorporating simulated halftoning and diffusion dithering in colour etchings, experimenting with different resolutions to achieve a dot-size small enough to show detail, but large enough to etch. By 'colourising' the layers of a digital image and adjusting their transparency, Hodes is able to obtain a prior indication of the most promising combinations of colours for multi-impression prints. Each layer, or combined layers, can be copied to create a new image, which is then converted to black and white for film output.

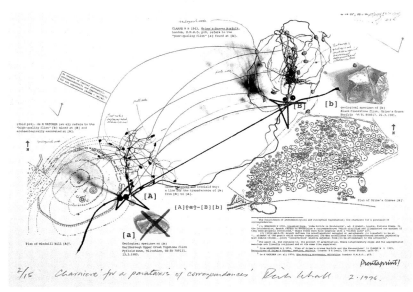

Charnière for a parataxis of correspondences, Dick Whall, UK, 1993–1996. Digitised print-assembly, 29.5 x 42cm (11.6 x 16.5in.).

For sheer inventiveness in combining digital and non-digital media, it would be difficult to beat Dick Whall. His print *Charnière for a parataxis of correspondences* involved photographing the shadows cast by an intricate miniature construction, and collaging the photograph with scanned images of archaeological site diagrams and drawings of geological specimens, to create an edition of photocopies, finally overprinted with an etched image, in red.

Using toner transfer paper (e.g. Lazertran)

With transfer paper and heat, it is possible to transfer a black and white laser print directly to an intaglio plate without the need for any photographic process. The printing side of the transfer paper has a glossy, water-soluble coating to receive the toner image, which must be a negative of the image on screen (use Photoshop: *Image –>Adjust–>Invert*, or equivalent command). The paper is thin enough to pass through the laser printer (it may need to be hand-fed – check with printer manufacturer), although care must be taken to keep the surface clean and dry.

Placed face-down on a degreased zinc or copper etching plate, heat is applied to the reverse side of the paper, preferably using a heat transfer press, although it is possible to use a domestic iron in combination with a thin metal cover plate (to spread the heat). Some experimentation is needed to determine the optimum temperature and time needed to melt the toner; normally it will be around 350°F for 30 or 40 seconds. When cool, water is sponged onto the paper, which is then peeled off. The etching plate, left to dry then placed onto a hot plate to ensure all toner has

The Evening, Rodica Simon, USA, 1998. Etching/aquatint, 39.4 x 24.8cm (15.5 x 9.75in.). A digital image was first created as a set of overlaid, spot colour 'channels', which were then individually laser printed onto sheets of toner transfer paper. Each printing plate was prepared by placing a sheet face down on the plate and heating, causing the toner to melt and adhere to the plate, creating an acid-resistant mask.

adhered, is ready for aquatint/etching. Very large images can be made by carefully taping together sections of a tiled print.

In addition to transfer paper for etching, Lazertran provide toner transfer papers for affixing colour laser prints to any surface – paper, glass, stone, wood, metal, plastic. Full instructions for use are given on their website (see Supplies and Services).

Digital *chine collé*

UK artist Angie Rogers has devised a technique to facilitate multicolour *chine collé* work. After proofing, an etching plate (with a little ink left on it, for visibility) is scanned, horizontally reflected (Photoshop: *Image–>Rotate Canvas–>Flip Horizontal*), and used as a guide for placement of coloured elements on a superimposed (digital) image layer. This second layer is inkjet printed onto thin paper, using water-resistant inks. The inkjet print, after trimming, is dampened, lightly glued, and placed face-down on the inked plate in the usual way for *chine collé*.

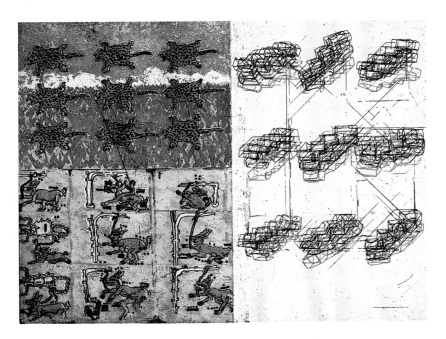

Freedom and Imprisonment, Isaac Victor Kerlow, USA, 1986. Colour etching and drypoint, 48 x 67cm (19 x 26.5in.). The right hand section was engraved directly into a copper plate using a pen plotter in which the pen had been replaced by a steel needle.

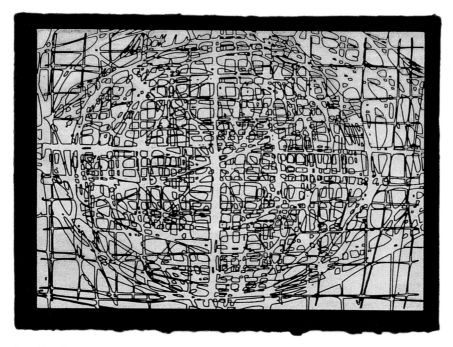

Graphic Primitives 1, Terry Winters, USA, 1998. Woodcut in two colours on Japanese Kochi paper, 52.1 x 66cm (20.5 x26in.). One of a portfolio of nine prints. Original drawings were scanned and digitally reworked, vectorised, and supplied as CorelDRAW files. A laser engraving machine cut the images into cherry wood blocks – each image was printed in white oil paint from the block and wiped with black Yasutomo Sumi ink. According to David Lasry (Two Palms Press, New York) who editioned the portfolio, 'Hand carving each block would have taken months and even with enough time it was unlikely that we could maintain the pure mechanical perfection of the computer drawn lines.'

Monument, Paul Thirkell, UK, 1998. Digital collotype in seven colours, 34 x 30cm (13.4 x 11.8in.).

Automated cutting and engraving

Perhaps the simplest way to engrave a vector-based image directly is to place the metal plate on the bed of a flatbed plotter and replace the pen of the plotter by some kind of hard stylus. The right half of Victor Kerlow's *Freedom and Imprisonment* was engraved by this method. His steel needle, scratching through the hard ground and into the plate like a drypoint, kept sticking and 'jumping', unexpectedly creating 'lines with a beautiful quality'.

The low-tech way of transferring a digital image to a wood or lino block is simply to paste an inkjet or laser print to the block (much as one might do with a drawing), using it as a guide for manual cutting. The high-tech method involves a laser engraving machine, as used in industry for cutting and engraving precision components. There are two types of laser engraving: raster, and vector. In raster engraving, the laser head scans back and forth, engraving dots one line at a time into the material, like a dot-matrix printer: bitmapped images can be engraved at resolutions of up to around 1200 dpi, to almost any desired depth. Vector engraving, on the other hand, cuts vector images (e.g. from CorelDraw files) into, or right through, materials such as wood, acrylic and paper, and is normally used for such tasks as cutting inlays for the boating industry.

Digital collotype

Collotype is a nineteenth-century print process by which a bichromated gelatine plate is exposed to light under a negative to create a reticulated grain structure which, when inked, prints a fine-grained, almost continuous-tone image. An important feature of the process is its ability to produce rich, multicolour work without risk of *moiré* patterning. Paul Thirkell, of the Centre for Fine Print Research at the University of the West of England, has developed some impressive techniques for printing high-resolution digital images as collotypes (see previous page).

Grainer, Michael McGraw, UK, 1999. Collotype, 20 x 25cm (7.9 x 9.8in.). Image derived from an infra-red photograph of a lithographic plate-graining machine, scanned, inverted into negative, and imageset. The resulting film was UV-exposed in contact with the collotype plate.

Chapter 6
SCREENPRINTING AND LITHOGRAPHY

▮ Colour halftoning

Four-colour halftoning is the process which enables continuous-tone colour imagery to be reproduced using just four colours. Colour halftones are everywhere, in newspapers and magazines, on billboards, and on many of the enticingly-designed packages to be found in supermarkets. Most are produced by screenprinting or offset litho.

Magnified, such prints are seen to consist of patterns of tiny dots of cyan,

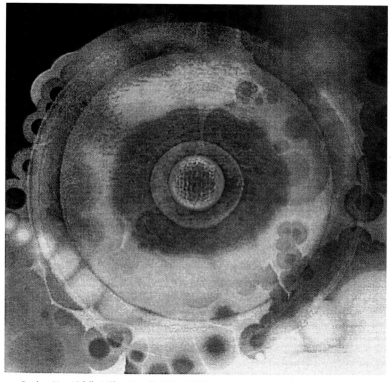

Planet Series No 13(d), Mike North, UK, 1995. Screenprint and watercolour, 25.4 x 25.4cm (10 x 10in.). Morphed images and fractal forms were combined and output as four-colour separations. Colour adjustments were made during manual screenprinting, and watercolour added to the finished print.

magenta, yellow and black ink, varying in size according to local image colour. Photographic methods have traditionally been used to separate and screen (break up into dots) each of the four colours, but nowadays halftoning is largely done on the computer, using image manipulation software such as Photoshop, or specialist publishing applications such as QuarkXPress. The resulting output can take a number of forms, for example, low-grade black and white laser proofs, or high-resolution film separations from a Linotronic imagesetter. Modern 'computer-to-plate' systems, developed by companies such as Dupont, can output halftone separations directly to lithographic plates without the need for a film intermediary, and similarly in commercial screenprinting, halftoned images can now be applied to fast photo-stencils by direct laser scanning.

For the artist-printmaker, high-quality film output is recommended where image quality and accuracy of registration are critical, but for the cost-conscious artist or student, halftone separations printed onto film or paper by a good quality black and white laser printer or inkjet printer can be used instead. These are exposed onto plate or screen using a conventional UV exposure unit. Paper positives often give better density, but experimentation may be necessary to determine the optimum exposure (making the paper translucent by rubbing a small amount of vegetable oil into the reverse side can reduce exposure time).

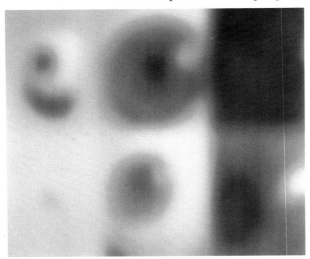

Eye, Grenville Davey, UK, 1993. Screenprint, 72 x 84cm (28.3 x 33in.). *Eye* is a set of three pairs of prints editioned by Coriander Studio in conjunction with After Image, London.
This print is from pair *A*. Photographs of a glass eye and a glass bottle stopper were combined, and a Gaussian blur applied. Output separations were used to make screens, which the artist edited.

'Stochastic' halftoning (much the same as dithering) is characterised by irregular distributions of dots, avoiding the rosette patterns associated with conventional four-colour halftoning. Adam Lowe of Permaprint, London, used stochastic separations for his portfolio *Digital Prints*, a comprehensive, comparative study of the surface qualities of prints made by many different processes, both modern and traditional. (Copies of *Digital Prints* are available for inspection in a number of important collections worldwide.)

Digital screenprinting

Simplifying the colour palette

The distinguishing quality of screenprinting is its ability to print broad, dense areas of colour onto just about any surface. A major concern when adapting a digital image for screenprinting is to reduce the number of colours, as each requires its own screen. When painting an image interactively, this is best achieved by restricting the palette right from the start. Scanned images, on the other hand, can be simplified using a posterisation filter, or by converting to indexed colour.

The next stage is to output the image in a form suitable for transfer to one or more screens. There are two methods, depending on whether the screen is to be made from hand-cut stencil (or film), or from a set of positives to be transferred photographically to screens:

1. Making a simple line template from a pixel-mapped image, for stencil cutting:

- check that the dimensions of the digital image match the required print size;

- make a duplicate copy of the image and convert it to indexed colour (Photoshop: *Image–>Mode–>Indexed Color...*), specifying the number of colours; adjust colours if necessary (e.g. using Photoshop: *Image–>Adjust–>Hue/Saturation...*);

Dialog box for converting an RGB image to indexed colour (*Image–>Mode–>Indexed Color...*). The number typed into the *Colors* box sets the total number of colours, corresponding to the number of different screens that would be needed to screenprint the image. Zoomed view shows the effect of colour dithering (which should not be used when making line templates).

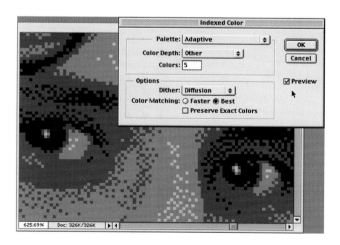

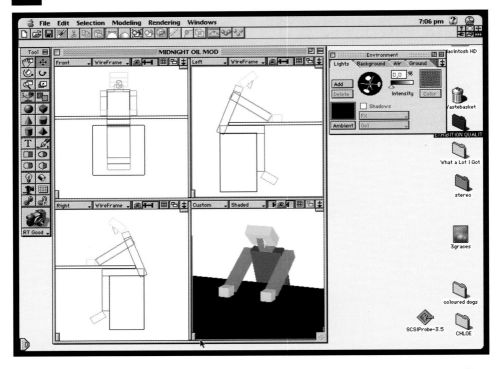

Front, left, right, and perspective views of a 3D model constructed in Strata Studio Pro by Jeffery Edwards.

- convert back to RGB, then apply an edge-detection filter (e.g. Photoshop: *Filter–>Stylize–>Find Edges*) so that only the boundaries between colour areas are shown; if the lines are too detailed, blur the image first;

- output the line image to inkjet or plotter, using inexpensive paper.

2. To make positives for photographic transfer, first convert the image to indexed colour as above, then for each colour:

- using the *Magic Wand* tool, or *Color Range* dialog box, select all parts of the image having that colour;

- copy and paste the selection to a new image of identical size;

- convert the new image to greyscale, then to black and white by max-imising contrast, and save the file;

- inkjet or laser print (with registration marks) onto clear film or thin paper;

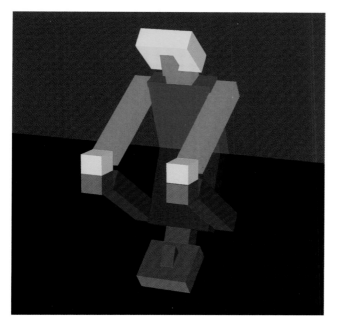

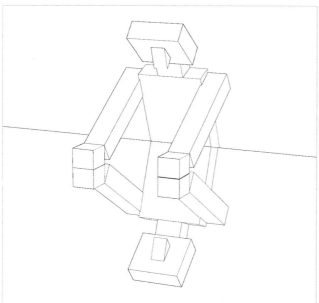

Midnight, Jeffery Edwards, UK, 1998. Edwards has successfully screenprinted 3D computer images onto large MDF panels, using cellulose-based inks. A high-resolution rendering (top) is first turned into a line-art template by application of an edge-detection filter, capturing the edges of cast shadows and reflections as well as the edges of the modelled objects themselves (bottom). Sheets of ruby film placed over the template can then be hand-cut to produce photo-positives, one for each colour.

SCREENPRINTING AND LITHOGRAPHY

Alone in London, Mônica Schoenacker, Brazil. Screenprint on needlework canvas, 60 x 50cm (23.6 x 19.7in.). A photograph taken near King's Cross station, London, was reduced to seven colours in Illustrator. Each colour was separately inkjet printed onto film, using black ink, to make a positive.

• if the density of the resulting positives is inadequate, a process camera may be used to copy them to high-density film; alternatively, the files may be imageset directly to film (see *Preparing Work for Professional Output* in Chapter 7).

The main problem in both cases is 'trapping' – ensuring just enough overlap between colours to ensure that shrinkage/expansion of film or paper, or slight mis-registration during printing, does not result in gaps, or 'halos'. In method 1, this is achieved manually; in method 2, the edges of each selection can be thickened by application of a 'stroke' of suitable width (e.g. Photoshop: *Edit–>Stroke...*). The use of opaque screen inks may facilitate overprinting, which can avoid the need for trapping altogether. Vector-based packages such as Illustrator contain special trapping features which can facilitate the creation of positives for screenprinting. In each case, a little experimentation may be called for.

Digital lithography

Most inkjet printers, although able to simulate 'classical' halftoning, achieve their best results by dithering, which accounts for the grainy appearance of some inkjet prints. Low-resolution black and white dithers

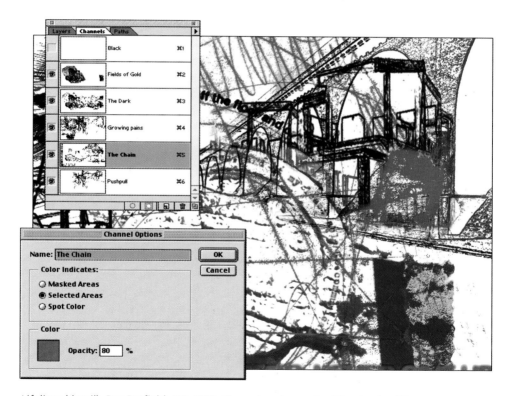

Lifelines (detail), Raz Barfield, UK, 1996. Five-colour image for lithography, 37 x 53cm (14.5 x 21 in.). 'Zoomed' region of a multi-channel image shows how the ordering of channels in the *Channels* palette, and the setting of colour and opacity in the *Channel Options* dialog box can be used to modify and visualise the effects of multiple, lithographic overprintings of spot colours. This kind of pre-visualisation is sometimes referred to as 'soft-proofing'.

can make excellent photo-positives for lithography, since the dots are large enough to be 'picked up', and their irregular distribution avoids the *moiré* effects that can arise with conventional colour halftones.

UK printmaker Raz Barfield has exploited this in the development of a unique process for the digital origination of multicolour lithographs. The process uses channels as the basis for image creation. A channel, containing imagery comprised of varying intensities of a single colour, is analogous to the printed impression made by a single plate. By adjusting the colour, transparency and ordering of channels, and seeing them superimposed in Photoshop, it becomes possible to simulate the effect of multiple overprintings of spot colour, and escape the restrictions of the CMYK colour gamut. Each image, which may contain several layers and up to ten channels, facilitates alternation between full-colour modifications to individual layers, and the painting or erasing of areas of individual channels to define areas of knockout or overprint.

Detail of *Lifelines* lithograph. Individual channels were output as paper positives, for transfer to photo-litho plates. The printer's native dithering capability gave the print a rich visual texture, with no hint of the *moiré* patterning that can arise when conventionally-halftoned separations are overlaid.

Using an ENCAD® Novajet III large-format printer, channels were separately output as (80 gsm) paper positives, used for exposing zinc photo-litho plates. (Positives for offset litho should be emulsion down: before printing, select Photoshop: *File–>Page Setup...*, then in the Photoshop settings, check *Emulsion Down*; alternatively, Photoshop: *Image–>Flip Horizontal*). Image files were saved in native Photoshop (PSD) file format to preserve layer/channel information for future reworking.

Chapter 7

PROFESSIONAL STUDIOS AND BUREAUX

■ Iris printing

Manufactured by Iris Graphics, Inc., Iris printers have been at the leading edge of fine art digital print editioning, able to produce prints with a perceived resolution of around 1800 dpi, and deep, saturated colours. The Iris 3047 and 3047G can print images up to 86.4 x 118.9cm (34 x 46.8in.) on sheets 88.9 x 119.4cm (35 x 47in.) in size, and precise registration makes it possible to 'double strike' an image to increase ink density.

Inside each Iris printer is a drum, to which a sheet of paper (or other substrate) is attached. The drum revolves at high speed whilst a print head, mounted on a stainless steel rod, passes in front of it. High-pressure

Marconi & Son, Richard Hamilton, UK, 1998. Iris print on Somerset, 53 x 69cm (20.9 x 27.2in.). (© Richard Hamilton 2000. All Rights Reserved, DACS.) Image created on Quantel Paintbox. Printed by Ian Cartwright at Circa, London.

Chelsea Arts Club, Eileen Hogan, UK, 2000. Inkjet, 50 x 50cm (19.7 x 19.7in.).

pumps supply ink to four inkjet nozzles housed in the print head. Each nozzle contains a quartz crystal which oscillates at a million cycles per second, breaking the ink supply into a continuous stream of tiny droplets. Passing through a charge tunnel, unwanted droplets are electrically charged and deflected away from the drum, whilst the remainder strike the substrate, combining to form variable-sized dots on the surface.

Translucent, dye-based CMYK ink sets for Iris printing include Iris Graphics Equipoise inks and the Fine Arts ink set made by Lyson. These are formulated to maximise lightfastness, and to achieve the broadest possible colour gamut, or range of printable colours. Special coatings are available to improve water and scuff resistance, or to increase lightfastness.

Iris printing has been successfully applied to a whole range of natural and synthetic substrates, but some of the most outstanding results have been achieved with traditional papers and supports, some of which have been adapted for inkjet through the incorporation of special emulsions or 'receivers' during manufacture, which combine with the inks to maximise colour saturation and image detail. Popular papers include Somerset Enhanced, in velvet, satin and textured finishes; fabrics include Milano Media Canvas and Iris Coated Cotton. (Lyson also manufacture a range of acid-free fine art papers for inkjet.)

The long-term *stability*, or permanency, of prints is an issue of particular importance to collectors. Rigorous scientific tests conducted by Henry Wilhelm (a recognised authority on the stability of digital and photographic colour images) have demonstrated that, depending on the particular combination of archival inks and paper used, colour prints will last for anything from 10 to 50 years in standard indoor display conditions before noticeable fading occurs, and monochrome (black only) prints can have much higher ratings, in excess of 100 years.

Orange Pants, Jim Dine, USA, 1999. Digital pigment print on canvas, 175 x 122cm (69 x 48in.). (Courtesy of Pace/MacGill Gallery, New York.)

David Adamson (foreground) and artist Chuck Close in the Adamson Editions studio. (Photograph courtesy of David Adamson.)

Digital ateliers

The last decade has seen remarkable growth in the number of professional studios, or ateliers, capable of editioning fine art digital prints – there are currently more than 200 such studios worldwide (around 90% in the US). Many of them use Iris technology, and it is largely through the pioneering work of Nash Editions, Cone Editions Press, Adamson Editions, Harvest Productions and other digital ateliers that Iris *giclée* 'prints' (from the French, *gicler*, 'to spray') have gained widespread acceptance.

Many ateliers undertake collaborative projects, where artist and master printmaker work closely in the development and proofing of an original

Untitled GF 4, Sue Gollifer, UK, 1999. Pigment transfer print, 48.3 x 48.3cm (19 x 19in.). Scanned textures were mapped onto geometric forms. (The pigment transfer process, first developed in the 1870s, uses gelatine sheets embedded with pigment to transfer process-colour separations to paper. The results are exceptionally stable.) Adam Lowe, of Permaprint, London, produced this print from computer-generated film separations of the digital original.

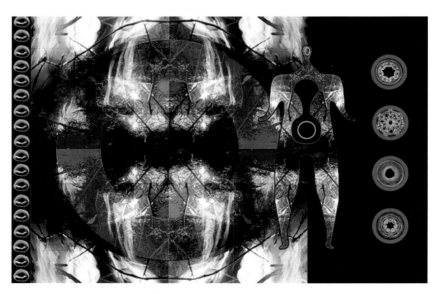

Fire Mandala, Martin Rieser, UK, 1996. Novajet print, 24 x 32 in. Image created for an ArtAids project entitled *Screening the Virus.*

image. Once approved, the final proof, or BAT (*Bon à tirer*) may be archived, together with print files and related set-up information, so that the edition can be printed as and when needed ('print-on-demand'). Most studios also offer faster, less expensive facilities for printing supplied images using standard materials and formats.

Adamson Editions (Washington, D.C.) was founded in 1994 by David Adamson, a classically trained printmaker formerly of the Slade School of Art and the Tamarind Institute. Committed to the integration of digital technology into the vocabulary of printmaking, he has undertaken many successful and innovative collaborations with internationally renowned artists. In a project with Jim Dine, a wall decorated with poems provided the backdrop for studied arrangements of objects, which the artist photographed using the studio's high-resolution, 4 x 5 inch digital camera.

Underground (detail), Naren Barfield, UK, 1999. Installation, 61 x 61 x 213cm (24 x 24 x 84in.) high. More than 100 photographs of a London Underground station were 'stitched' together on the computer, inkjet printed, and pasted onto panels to facilitate torchlit exploration of the interior of the installation – a 360° 'cubic panorama'.

Absolut Bar-Min-Ski, Bill Barminski, USA, 1998. Inkjet on vinyl, 6.1 x 18.3m (20 x 60ft). A long-running billboard advertisement on Sunset Strip, Los Angeles. The martini glass moves up and down, the eyes move, stars twinkle, and the neon signs are real. (Under permission by V&S Vin and Sprit AB. ABSOLUT, the bottle design and seal are trademarks owned by V&S Vin and Sprit AB.)

Elements of the resulting images were layered, merged, and finally output as Roland HiFi prints (see pages 19 and 89).

Research by Mike Brown of Hunter Editions has revealed that annual spending by collectors on digital prints (mainly Irises) now runs into hundreds of millions of dollars. It was in response to rapid growth during the 1990s that the International Association of Fine Art Digital Printmakers (IAFADP) was set up to encourage and support the development of the fine art digital printmaking industry. Members include artists, photographers, editioners, gallery owners, manufacturers and publishers from around the world, and the IAFADP is an invaluable source of up-to-date information (see Other Information Sources for contact details).

Preparing work for professional output

An alternative to fine art editioners are commercial bureaux, advertised in computer magazines or yellow pages, able to print large-format indoor and outdoor signs, posters, and banners using different kinds of (usually non-archival) materials, or specialising in the production of high-resolution film output, colour transparencies and photographic prints.

Whether sending work to an editioner or to a graphics bureau, the cost of the first print may be significantly higher than the cost of subsequent prints, since it includes set-up and proofing charges. Another factor affecting cost is the amount of time spent optimising or adapting the supplied print file, so it is always worth seeking advice first on 'prepping' – preparing work for output. The following guidelines are generally applicable:

• right at the beginning of any project, check that the bureau is able to print to the required size and quality; if pixel-mapped images are to be output, find out the preferred resolution (pixels per inch), and set up the images accordingly;

- find out what kinds of disks are acceptable (e.g. Mac formatted Zip), and the preferred file types (e.g. TIFF or EPS);

- convert colour images (duotone, indexed colour, etc.) to RGB;

- do not convert from RGB to CMYK unless the bureau requests it – most have their own conversion methods designed to maximise colour gamut;

- delete any unnecessary channels (and delete paths, if any);

- if images *have* to be compressed to fit on disk, use a lossless compression method (e.g. LZW compressed TIFF) to avoid damaging the image;

- when supplying vector artwork (e.g. Illustrator files), place a background-coloured box in the background, filling the document setup area, otherwise the image may be cropped;

- if a file contains fonts and imported images, include these on the disk;

- if imagesetting to film, specify emulsion side up or down (similarly if printing onto clear film);

Miss Tracy, John Hilliard, UK, 1994. Scanachrome on vinyl, 252 x 210cm (99.2 x 82.7in.). Hilliard's use of the Scanachrome process, by which acrylic inks are sprayed onto very large sheets (of canvas, vinyl, leather, etc.) makes reference 'to the cinema screen, the advertising hoarding, and large-scale painting'. (Courtesy of Lisson Gallery, London.)

PROFESSIONAL STUDIOS AND BUREAUX

From the Silicon Age – fig 1.3, Anna Munster, Australia, 2000. Lambda print, 110 x 100cm (43 x 39in.). Textures derived from photographs and lithographs were applied to a 3D model constructed in Infini-D. This is one of a series of four images using seventeenth and eighteenth century forms of natural history illustration to depict 'the kinds of artifacts from our current silicon age that a natural historian of the future might ponder over.'

- always request a small-scale proof (printed using the same process and materials as the final print will be), to verify colour accuracy and image placement before proceeding with the final print or edition; this is especially important when an RGB image is to be output to a CMYK device, as images containing colours beyond the CMYK gamut will lose saturation when printed.

After double-checking that all necessary files are on the disk (which should be clearly labelled), send it to the bureau in a well-padded package, together with a reference print (can be black and white), and a written order specifying the name(s) of the file(s) to be printed, the final print size, substrate size and type, required completion date and contact number, should any problems arise. And keep back-up copies of everything, just in case!

Grand-format printing

Used in conjunction with specialist CAS (computer-aided sign-making) software, grand-format printers are designed to output billboard-size images for signs, banners and murals. Many of these devices utilise relatively low-resolution airbrush, or 'atomising', systems with digitally-controlled traversing spray heads able to deposit ink or paint onto many kinds of substrates, including paper, vinyl and fabric. Others use piezo inkjet, or laser technology. Specialist producers often have in-house

4 intervals, Tim O'Riley, UK, 1998. Durst Lambda C-type print, 80 x 152cm (31.5 x 59.8in.).

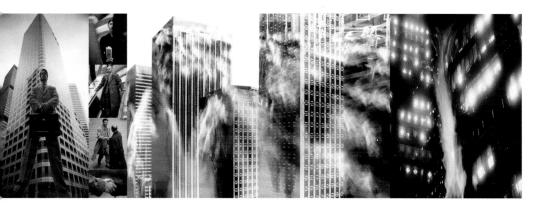

The Fireman, Jane Prophet, UK, 1999. Three panels, each 322 x 220cm (127 x 87in.). Printed on transparent Duratran, this image was created for the exterior of Lux Gallery, London, using stock photographs supplied by PhotoDisc®. 'From outside the piece glowed at night like an advert'.

facilities for laminating prints onto rigid supports (plastic, aluminium, etc.) and some give 'outdoor-use' warranties – typically two to three years.

The WIREJET™ PM1500 printer is a vertical flatbed printer which uses a paint injection technology for continuous tone printing up to 6m (20 ft) wide on most flexible or rigid media. The manufacturers, Friend or Faux Technologies (US), claim that it can print using most kinds of paint, including acrylic, oil, and household gloss.

The VUTEk UltraVu series of grand-format, drop-on-demand, piezo inkjet printers use pigmented, solvent-based inks suited for vinyl and other substrates destined for outdoor use. The latest models are six-colour.

Digital laser imaging machines such as the Lambda 130 made by Durst Phototechnik use red, green and blue lasers to transfer digital images directly onto rolls of photographic media up to 127cm (50in.) wide. Media include paper, Duratran (for backlighting), Duraclear (for mounting onto glass or perspex), and vinyl.

Online marketing

Art is increasingly being marketed and sold online. GUILD.com, for example, based in Madison, Wisconsin, boasts an impressive website containing thousands of original prints. The photographic origin of many of the digital prints in their collection reflects the high level of interest amongst photographers in *giclée* processes. Many individual artists are also setting up their own websites for marketing and selling prints.

Barbara Seidel
Click Artist Name for More Information

"Kitchenwork #5"
An unframed iris print on heavy somerset paper. The print is created from an original photograph by the artist, scanned on an HP scanner, manipulated on a Macintosh computer and then outputted to an iris printer. Signed, numbered and dated by the artist. Limited edition of six.

Dimensions: 22"H x 17"W
Limited Edition
Item: AI1474-3
Special Information: Printed on 22" x 17" paper.

Shipping & Handling: $10

Enlarge
ADD TO MY COLLECTION
My Collection is your personal space for storing your GUILD.com favorites.

Price: $350
BUY
To add this item to your basket, click Buy.

Quantity Desired: 1

Web page from GUILD.com, one of the new online art marketing sites. (Courtesy of GUILD.com. Artwork © Barbara Seidel.)

Chapter 8
SOFTWARE AS A CREATIVE MEDIUM

■ The imaging techniques described in previous chapters have used 'off-the-shelf' applications. These applications are able to support a very broad range of tasks, but they all have their limits. After all, software designers can't be expected to predict all the quirky, idiosyncratic things that individual artists might want to do.

Faced with a situation in which none of the readily available applications can do the job, an artist has several options: to trawl the Internet, hoping that someone, somewhere, possesses exactly the piece of software required; failing that, to think of another way of doing things; finally, to modify the project, or abandon it altogether. Fortunately, there is a fourth option, which is for the artist to learn how to program, thereby gaining control over the inner workings of the computer, and greatly enhancing the potential for exploring new and potentially complex ideas. Programming is not a quick or easy option, but the necessary skills can be acquired by anybody with perseverance, regardless of age (some of the best artist-programmers are reassuringly mature).

Programming languages

Programming is a way of passing commands to the computer using a programming language, consisting of a limited vocabulary of key words and mathematical expressions. Programming languages, which tend to be much simpler than natural languages such as English or French (and far more logical) come in a range of acronyms, including BASIC (Beginners' All-purpose Symbolic Instruction Code), Fortran (Formula translation), and LISP (LISt Processing). Some are named after famous people, for example Ada, after Ada Lovelace, the world's first computer programmer, and some have odd names, for example C, and C++ (pronounced 'C plus plus'). Most of them can be used for making digital images, but C and BASIC are probably the most popular.

Strictly speaking, programming is only one aspect of software development, since the artist-programmer must first decide exactly what he/she wants the computer to do, and then work out a stepwise plan of action, or algorithm, which can be typed into the computer as source code, a sequence of statements in the chosen language. The computer runs the program, having converted the source code into low-level instructions, then displays the results; more often than not, the artist continues to correct and modify the program until, by accident or design, it produces some interesting pictures.

Monday Morning, Anna Ursyn, USA, 1994. Photo-silkscreen, 61 x 91.5cm (24 x 36 in.). Elements of this image were created by the artist's own software, written in the Fortran 77 programming language.

Drawing with Logo

Invented in 1967 by mathematician Seymour Papert as a teaching aid, the Logo language is based on simple principles, but is nevertheless a powerful tool for creating two-dimensional patterns and drawings, and has also been used in multimedia, mathematics, musical composition and robotics. Logo comes in different versions, including MicroWorlds Logo for Macintosh and PCLogo for Windows; shareware versions are also available. The Logo Foundation offers free information and support for Logo programming.

Imagine, if you will, a large sheet of paper, with a turtle standing on it, holding a pen (an unusual scenario, admittedly). The turtle can move forwards, drawing a line as he goes, and can be told to turn at any stage. To draw a 10-unit square (units might be pixels, centimetres, or inches), the turtle first has to be told to move forward 10 units, then turn 90 degrees to the right, then move forward 10, then turn right again, and so on until he arrives back at the starting point. This algorithm for drawing a square can be written as a Logo program:

```
forward 10
right 90
forward 10
right 90
forward 10
right 90
forward 10
right 90
```

The choice of a turtle for this onerous task might seem a little strange. In fact, it is possible to buy a robotic 'turtle' and program it to crawl about on a large sheet of paper, leaving a trail behind it. Normally, though, drawings are displayed on the computer screen, and can be output to a desktop printer, or saved as a disk file.

Since the same basic actions are repeated four times, the above commands can be reduced to a simple procedure:

```
to square
    repeat 4 [fd 10 rt 90]
end
```

where 'to' and 'end' indicate the start and end of the procedure, 'square' is

Logo drawings based on traditional African textiles, by students of Joan of Arc Junior High School, New York. Right: Asante design from Ghana (Michael Hailstock). Below: cotton textile design from Ebira, Nigeria (Myckele Spencer).
Simple procedures were used to draw the arrows, crosses and other constituent shapes.

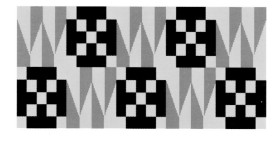

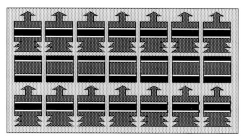

the name of the procedure, 'repeat 4' means 'repeat the following four times', and the square brackets contain the (abbreviated) commands to be repeated. Now the single command 'square' can be used instead of the original eight. Repetition, or iteration, is a key feature of most computer programs, as is conditional branching, which enables choices between alternative sequences of actions, and there are usually built-in commands for setting the colour, weight (width) and other attributes of the 'virtual pen'.

Advanced graphics programming

More ambitious programming usually requires a more powerful language such as Pascal, C, or C++. Such languages have built-in commands for drawing simple forms in various styles, and there are also libraries of ready-made procedures (or functions, as they are called in C) which can be linked to the programmer's own code, including libraries to facilitate the creation and manipulation of more complex 2D and 3D images. Special

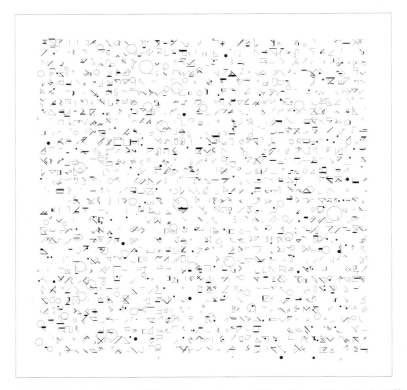

P-049/R, Manfred Mohr, 1970. Ink/paper/ wood, 100 x 100cm (39 x 39in.). Different line characteristics are used to make alphabets of arbitrary elements, where the creation and selection of elements is partly random.

packages called integrated development environments, or IDEs, provide suites of tools to facilitate program development. Popular IDEs include Visual C++ for Windows, and Code Warrior for the Mac. Introductory books on C, C++, and graphics programming are widely available, and most IDEs have good online help.

The programming approaches of the artists in the remainder of this chapter represent only a few of the possibilities. Some sources of information on shape grammars, evolutionary algorithms and other algorithmic image-generation techniques are given in Other Information Sources.

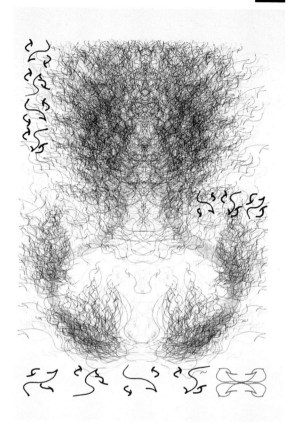

Geometric approaches

Much of the pioneering work in programmed art was vector-based, partly because the best available large-format output devices in the 1960s and 1970s

Diamond Lake Apocalypse (left-hand panel), Roman Verostko, USA, 1994. Multicolour plot using pens and brushes, 76 x 56cm (30 x 22in.).

were pen-plotters. The Algorists, a group of artists committed to making art with, or from, algorithms (in other words they create software to make art) include Charles Csuri and Roman Verostko, who were amongst the first to recognise and exploit the creative potential of large-format plotters.

For many years Roman Verostko has been developing detailed procedures, which he calls form generators, for initiating, developing and improvising an idea for 'growing an art form'. His works are executed with a multi-pen plotter using coloured inks mixed in the studio. Most drawings require thousands of lines and frequent pen changes, which are software controlled, and an optional brush routine allows the occasional substitution of a brush for a pen. A number of younger artists continue this tradition of abstract, vector-based work. Robert Urbásek, from Bratislava, makes monochromatic screenprints from dense, systematic line drawings that would be onerous, if not impossible, to do by hand.

Levitácia (Levitation), Robert Urbásek, Slovak Republic, 1997. Serigraph, 50 x 50cm (20 x 20in.).

Green Sonata, Ian Gordon, UK, 1998. Inkjet, 28 x 28cm (11 x 11in.). Image generated by the artist's own program, *Leonardo,* and printed on Epson coated paper.

Whereas Urbásek's prints consist of many individual lines positioned according to some algorithm, Ian Gordon's recent inkjet prints are derived from manipulated grid structures containing precisely controlled colour values. Describing programming as 'a very satisfying creative activity' that enables him to interact with the computer 'at a more primitive level', he selects the final images himself from large numbers of variants output by the program, acknowledging that it's still far easier to program a computer to generate art than to evaluate it.

Pixel-based approaches

Given that the colours of pixels in a pixel-map are represented internally as numbers, it is possible to devise algorithms systematically to change these colours, an approach adopted by a number of artists.

Joseph Nechvatal, in collaboration with Jean-Philippe Massonie, has developed a computer program which erodes and mutates image files. He scanned his entire body of previous work into the computer, then exposed it to the 'virus' program, with fascinating, sometimes disturbing results.

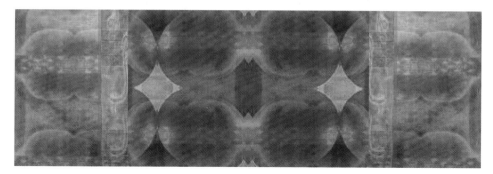

OCOMPLIANT, Joseph Nechvatal, France, 2000. Mutated pixel-map, 150 x 432 pixels.

Experiments in halftoning

In recent years, there has been much research in the field of 'non-photorealistic rendering', techniques for depicting scanned images or 3D computer models in more artistic ways. Programs developed by computer scientists are able to break down pixel-maps into black and white line images reminiscent of traditional engravings or pen and ink drawings, and are potentially of great interest to the printmaker since they offer ways of reducing a greyscale or full-colour image into one or more separations that can be used for printing.

Following the scientists' lead, some print artists have developed their own forms of halftoning using digital dots, lines or shapes and unconstrained by the need for precise tonal reproduction, they are often

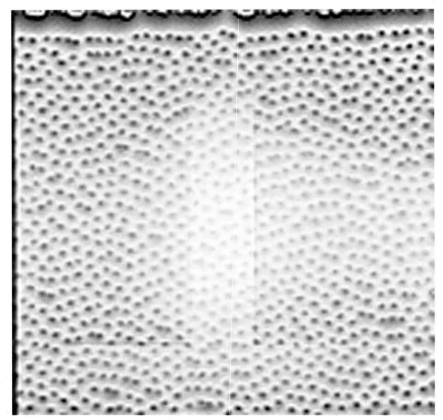

CodeZoneLight200, Douglas Sheerer, Australia, 1999. Algorithmically generated pixel-map. Sheerer likens his code to musical notation: 'a time based drawing awaiting its proper translation and rendition'.

Non-photorealistic (NPR) 'streamline' rendering of a 3D model (detail), Rich Coutts, USA, 1997. The lines follow surface contours, and vary in density to show tone.

Digital Facial Engraving (detail), Victor Ostromoukhov, Canada, 1999. An example of non-photorealistic rendering (NPR), inspired by traditional engraving techniques. Different engraving 'styles' can be stored and applied to 2D source images.

Underpass, George Whale, UK, 1996. Inkjet, 45 x 66cm (18 x 26in.). Greyscale image halftoned using randomised line segments.

Cycladic Figure, Naren Barfield, UK, 1999. Inkjet, 259 x 137cm (102 x 54 in.).
'Autographic halftone', printed with a Hewlett-Packard 3500CP large-format printer.

John Glenn, Charles Csuri, USA, 1998. Screen-shot from an interactive VRML artwork.

able to be looser, or more expressive. The lower image on page 105 was created by replacing the pixels of a 2D image by lines whose width and distribution vary according to local image density.

A different approach was taken by Naren Barfield. Keen to retain an autographic quality, he decided to use sets of artist-made marks and shapes, appropriately scaled and positioned and augmented by new forms generated by 'in-betweening', or interpolating, pairs of the original marks. *Cycladic Figure* (opposite) which combines several layers of 'autographic halftones' derived from the same pixel-map, was inkjet printed in sections, to a height of more than 8 feet.

Scripts and visual languages

An alternative to conventional programming languages such as C are graphical scripting languages which, although relatively easy to learn, provide powerful, high-level commands for image creation and manipulation. They include HTML (Hypertext Markup Language) which is mainly used to create text and graphics for web pages, and VRML (Virtual Reality Modelling Language) for building 3D environments. Many popular imaging applications have their own scripting languages. Photoscripter, for example, can be used to program sequences of actions in Photoshop, such as making selections, applying filters, creating new layers,

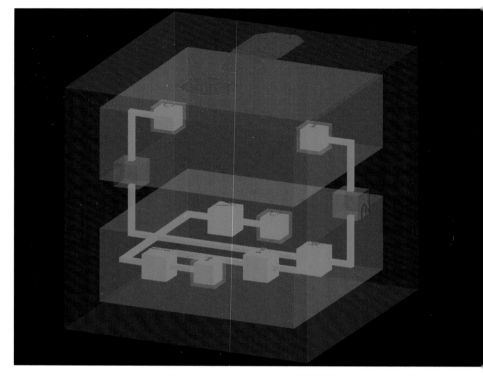

Factorial, Marc Najork, USA, 1993. Cube is an experimental 3D visual programming language – programs consist of arrangements of three-dimensional shapes instead of text.

changing pixel colours, or manipulating *Bézier* paths.

A fundamental problem with computer programs and scripts is that they are essentially one-dimensional, consisting of sequences of statements built from a limited vocabulary. This is hardly the most natural way for visual artists to express themselves. As a result, some artists have sought specialist help, and some of the pieces reproduced in this chapter are the result of collaborations between artists and software experts. Long term, the best solution might be to make programming itself more visual, and there are already visual programming languages (VPLs) on the market, enabling a user to originate a program entirely by interaction with graphical elements displayed on-screen. At present, representations tend to be diagrammatic – flow charts, graphs and so on – but visually richer programming environments might eventually become available, encouraging more artists to seek creative expression through software.

Chapter 9

PRINTMAKING IN THE AGE OF GLOBAL COMMUNICATION

■ New collaborations

In 1996, in conjunction with the exhibition *New Concepts in Printmaking*, the Museum of Modern Art in New York acquired a set of nine digital images from artist Peter Halley, which became the basis of an interactive website entitled *Exploding Cell*. By simply pointing and clicking, a visitor to the site can create an 'original' print by randomising the colours of a selected image, placing their own name alongside the artist's signature, and outputting the result.

More interesting collaborative possibilities are suggested by *Generation/Mutation*, a 'sitework' that first went online in May 1998. Artists are invited to choose a source image, download it, modify it in any

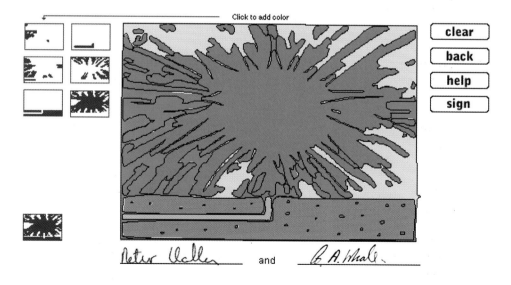

Exploding Cell, Peter Halley and George Whale, USA & UK, 1997–2000. Colour laser print, 14 x 25cm (5.5 x 9.8in.). Created and printed from an interactive online project developed by Peter Halley and Charles Carrico for the website of the Museum of Modern Art, New York. (Courtesy of MoMA.)

way they see fit, and return it with a new title. Modified images themselves become available for further alteration, resulting in a 'tree' of variant images, each the work of any number of artists from around the world.

Concurrent collaboration, whereby geographically separate groups of specialists work together on a project, at the same time, is facilitated by

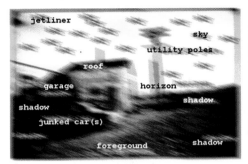

Generation/Mutation, concept by H-Ray Heine, USA, 2000. Images derived from the same source are successively modified. (Clockwise from top-left): *Deconstruction #7*, H-Ray Heine; *Moon Valley Wedding*, Carl Patzel; *A New Life*, Polina; *The Death Mask of Justin Timberlake*, Daniel C. Boyer.

technical developments in electronic communication, and looks likely to become increasingly popular with visual artists.

The virtual museum

Whilst fine art digital prints are gaining acceptance in traditional venues, fresh opportunities for exhibiting, marketing and selling prints are being created by the Internet. Moreover, research into reusable 'digital papers', and flexible, wafer-thin display technologies may eventually make traditional media obsolescent. Scientists at Cambridge Display Technology (UK) have already developed such displays using light-emitting polymers (LEPs) – Seiko-Epson have developed a technique for inkjet printing them.

Prints can now be duplicated, distributed and transformed quickly and easily, to become part of what William J. Mitchell called the 'complex

Mark Dysillabic 1916: Famous German chess player, Claudia Probst and Michael Shpaizman, Germany, 1996. From the *Digital Mutations* website; one of a series of 'virtual relatives'; strange, sometimes disturbing conjunctions of traditional family portraits and computer-generated textures.

networks of interconnection between images', and no amount of regulation, or digital watermarking (the use of special software to embed invisible copyright information into an image) can fully resolve the complex issues of ownership raised, or the difficulties of archiving and cataloguing such material for posterity.

Martin Rieser, who in 1989 curated *The Electronic Print*, the first British exhibition of prints created by computers, recently identified the problem: 'The Fine Print', he said, 'remains a deeply conservative concept at odds with the instant transmissive ubiquity of the digital image'.

The future

This book has shown some of the innovative ways in which artists have utilised computers in the making of original prints. Future technological developments and the creative processes and products that may arise from them, can only be guessed at, but we can be fairly confident that digital printmaking will continue to change and diversify – becoming less a definable set of practices, more a means by which visual artists can connect to, and exploit, a broad range of computer-based technologies.

Insofar as artists and editioners remain open to new technical possibilities and new forms of creative collaboration, the prospects are bright. Printmaking may yet retain its own distinct identity, or may continue to question its own boundaries in the light of continued technological and conceptual development, and forge a new identity. As Joann Moser, Senior Curator at the Smithsonian American Art Museum has pointed out, 'Whether that identity is a positive one, distinguished by stimulating ideas, or a negative one, marked by technical concerns, will determine whether printmaking thrives as a medium of artistic expression'. As ever, the crucial components are the creativity and ideas of the artists themselves.

GLOSSARY

A0, A1, A2, A3, A4, A5, A6
See *paper sizes*.

All-digital print
Print made by a computer-controlled output device, without recourse to traditional, non-digital methods.

Anti-aliasing
A smoothing technique used to eliminate jaggedness of lines and edges in pixel-mapped images.

Archival materials
Inks and *substrates* designed for long-term stability.

Archiving
Storage (usually on CD) of a *print file*, materials specifications and *hardware* and *software* settings; important where an edition is to be printed over several sessions.

Banding
Consequence of having too few colours to give a smooth blend.

Bézier curve (or path)
A type of mathematically-defined, smooth curve used in *vector-based* drawing.

Bit (binary digit)
Smallest unit of data.

Bits per pixel
The number of *bits* needed to represent the colour of a single *pixel* – a measure of the precision with which colour is represented in a digital image, e.g. 1-bit, 8-bit, 24-bit.

Byte
Group of 8 *bits*.

Channel, alpha
Extra channel used for selective masking of parts of a *pixel-mapped* image.

Channel, colour
Separate representation of one of the colour components of a *digital image*, e.g. red, green, blue for an *RGB* image.

Channel, spot
Channel whose colour is user-defined.

CMYK
See *colour models*.

Coating
Applied to a *substrate* during manufacture or prior to printing to improve print quality, or after printing to improve scuff and water resistance.

Colour gamut
The range, or 'space', of colours that can be represented by a *colour model*, or produced by a print process.

Colour models (colour modes, colour spaces)
Systems for specifying colour, for example RGB (red, green, blue, the additive primaries), CMYK (cyan, magenta, yellow, black, the process colours), HSV (hue, saturation, value), HLS (hue, lightness, saturation), and HWB (hue, whiteness, blackness); each system has a particular *colour gamut*.

Colour profile
Used in colour management, profiles describe the colour characteristics of individual devices, facilitating accurate translation of colour from one device to another.

Combination print (hybrid print)
The result of using digital output in combination with traditional print-making methods.

Compression
Encoding of data to reduce *file* size; compression may be 'lossy' (e.g. JPEG file compression), giving small files with some image degradation, or lossless (e.g. LZW compression of TIFF files), giving larger files with no degradation.

Continuous-tone (contone)
The term used to describe images, such as photographs or very high resolution prints, which have no apparent grain or structure to them, hence a smooth transition from one tone to another.

Cutting plotter
Plotter with a cutting head, used mainly in the sign industry for cutting *vector-based* images out of vinyl and other substrates.

Digital camera
Camera which stores images on magnetic media instead of film, so that they can be downloaded directly to a computer via a cable.

Digital halftone
Digitally-made halftone: AM (amplitude-modulated) screening places *pixel* clusters on a regular grid to simulate the different dot sizes of photographic halftones; FM (frequency-modulated) screening, or 'dithering', uses alternative patterns of pixel distribution to represent the continuous tones of an image, and is the method usually employed by digital print devices.

Digital image
An image in digital form (see *pixel-mapped image, vector image*).

Digital print
All-digital print, or *combination print*.

Dithering, dither pattern
See *digital halftone*.

Dot gain
Increase in size of a printed dot resulting from a particular combination of *ink* and *substrate*.

DPI (dots per inch)
A measure of the spatial resolution of a printer or other output device (also: dots per centimetre).

Driver
Program controlling a device such as a *scanner* or printer.

Dye-sublimation printer
Output device in which solid, dye-based *ink* is sublimated (converted to gas), re-solidifying on contact with the *substrate* to give the effect of *continuous tone*.

Electrostatic printer
Large-format device that works in a similar way to a colour photocopier.

Feathering
The blurring of the edges of a selected area of a *pixel-mapped* image.

File
A set of data stored on disk; image files normally comprise a 'header', defining image dimensions, colour palette, etc., followed by the image data itself which may be compressed.

File format
A way of storing digital information in a *file*. Common formats include TIFF and JPEG formats for *pixel-mapped images*, EPS for *vector-based images*, and DXF for 3D models. Most applications also have their own native formats.

Firewire™
High-bandwidth connector for rapidly transmitting large amounts of data between devices. Particularly used for digital video.

Giclée
A fine art *inkjet* print (from the French *gicler*, 'to spray').

Gigabyte (GB)
1024 *megabytes*.

Grand-format
Ultra-large, billboard-sized printing.

Hardware
Equipment, including the computer, monitor, printer and other peripheral devices.

HiFi (high fidelity) Printing
Use of six *inks* instead of the usual four process colours to increase colour *gamut* and/or print quality, e.g. Pantone® Hexachrome, which comprises CMYK plus orange and green.

HLS
See *colour models*.

HSV
See *colour models*.

Imagesetter
Thermal or laser device for producing high-*resolution*, black and white output on film or paper.

Indexed colour image
Image in which each *pixel* value is a number, or index, representing an actual (*RGB*) colour stored in a colour look-up table (CLUT); limited to 256 colours or less, so generally unsuitable for *continuous-tone*.

Ink, dye-based
Ink whose colour derives from dissolved dyes; most *inkjet printers* currently use dye-based ink.

Ink, pigment-based
Ink whose colour derives from tiny suspended particles of pigment; generally more lightfast than *dye-based ink*, but with a smaller *colour gamut*.

Inkjet printer
Non-contact print device which works by spraying streams of tiny *ink* droplets through nozzles: bubblejet printers use heat expansion to create the driving pressure; others use piezo-electric or air pressure.

Internet
Worldwide network of computers enabling instant exchange of images, documents, etc.

Interpolation
When enlarging an image by increasing the number of *pixels*, interpolation is the process by which new pixels are computed from existing ones.

IRIS print
Print made with an IRIS *inkjet* printer.

Laser printer
Device in which a laser beam is used to transfer an electrical charge-pattern of an image onto a drum; the drum is rolled through pigmented toner, picking up toner in the charged areas, and finally fusing it to the *substrate* by heat and pressure.

Layer
An image plane, like a sheet of acetate.

Lossy/lossless
See *compression*.

LPI (lines per inch)
Number of lines of variable-sized halftone dots per inch in a halftone screen.

Megabyte (MB)
1024 kilobytes (kilobyte = 1024 *bytes)*. The size of an image *file* may be given in MB, indicating the amount of space it will take up in the computer's memory (RAM), or on disk.

Moiré
A *moiré* pattern is the visible (and usually undesirable) pattern created by the interference between different screened parts of an image.

Paper sizes
A0 = 33.6 x 47.5in.; A1 = 23.8 x 33.6in.; A2 = 16.8 x 23.8in.; A3 = 11.9 x 16.8in.; A4 = 8.4 x 11.9in.; A5 = 5.9 x 8.4in.; A6 = 4.2 x 5.9in.

PDL (Page Description Language)
Object-based language for describing text and images on a page, e.g. Adobe PostScript and Hewlett-Packard PCL (Printer Control Language).

Photo-CD
A CD-ROM containing image *files*, usually in several different *resolutions*, derived from conventional photographs.

Pixel (picture-element)
One of the tiny dots that make up a displayed *digital image.*

Pixel-mapped image (pixel-map or raster image)
An image represented in the computer as a grid, or matrix, of *pixel* values. The terms bit-mapped image, or bitmap, are sometimes used instead, but really apply only to monochrome (1-bit) images (see *bits per pixel*).

Plotter (pen-plotter)
Flatbed or drum device for outputting line drawings onto paper or film by means of pens attached to a moving head.

PPI (pixels per inch)
A measure of the spatial resolution, the level of detail, of a *pixel-mapped image.*

Print file
Image *file* used for final proofing and editioning.

Print-on-demand
The production of the individual prints of an edition (from an archived *print file*) as and when needed.

RAM (Random Access Memory)
The computer's memory – where programs and data are stored whilst in use.

Rasterisation
Software conversion of a *vector image* into *pixels* or dots (see *RIP*).

Resampling (downsampling)
Reducing the number of *pixels* in an image, with corresponding loss of information. Sometimes applied also to *interpolation*.

Resolution
See *DPI, LPI, PPI*.

RGB
See *colour models*.

RIP (raster image processor)
Device/*software* for converting a *digital image* into a suitably sized matrix, or raster, of colour values for output to a large-format printer.

Scanner
Flatbed or drum device used to convert a drawing, photograph, transparency or other source material into a *pixel-mapped image*.

SCSI (small computer systems interface)
A standard system for connecting devices (hard drives, removable media, *scanners*, etc.) to a computer. Now largely superseded by *USB*.

Simulated halftone See *digital halftone*.

Software
Computer programs (also: packages, applications).

Solid inkjet printer
Output device using solid, wax-based *inks* which are melted before transfer to the *substrate*.

Stability
Resistance of a print to degradation over time by light, or environmental factors; data on the stability of particular combinations of *ink* and *substrate* are obtainable from reputable manufacturers.

Substrate
Surface onto which an image is printed, e.g. *inkjet* paper, traditional print-making paper, canvas or plastic.

Thermal-transfer printer
Output device that works by transferring *ink* from coated rolls or ribbons in contact with the *substrate*.

Tile (panel)
When an image is too large to be printed on a single sheet, some imaging and page layout packages can subdivide it into rectangular regions, or tiles, which are printed individually.

USB (Universal Serial Bus)
Type of connector for attaching peripheral devices to PC and Mac computers.

Vector image (vector-based image)
An image represented in the computer as a set of geometric entities – points, lines and shapes with specified attributes.

Vectorisation
Software conversion of a *pixel-mapped image* into a *vector image*.

ABOUT THE AUTHORS

George Whale graduated in Fine Art from Portsmouth Polytechnic in 1983, obtained his masters degree in Computing in Design from Middlesex Polytechnic in 1989, and has worked both in the commercial printing industry, and in the field of software engineering. His research into digital printmaking has been widely published, and he continues to exhibit digital prints internationally. He is currently a researcher at Loughborough University School of Art and Design, UK, engaged in the computational modelling of aspects of creative drawing.

    george_whale@yahoo.com

Dr Naren Barfield is an artist. He studied fine art at St. Martin's School of Art and Camberwell College of Arts, where he also completed his PhD in digital printmaking. His work has been exhibited internationally, and his research interests include the spatial and drawing applications of digitally-mediated art, which have been published widely. He is currently Senior Lecturer in Fine Art: Print at Wimbledon School of Art, and uses Apple computers - oh yes!

    nbarfield@Wimbledon.ac.uk

BIBLIOGRAPHY

Adobe Photoshop for Photographers, by Martin Evening (Focal Press).
The Computer in the Visual Arts, by Anne Morgan Spalter (Addison Wesley).
Creative Digital Printmaking: A Photographer's Guide to Professional Desktop Printing, by Theresa Airey (Watson-Guptill).
Fundamental Photoshop: A Complete Introduction, by Adele Droblas Greenberg and Seth Greenberg (Osborne/McGraw-Hill).
The Non-Designer's Scan and Print Book, by Sandee Cohen and Robin Williams (Peachpit Press).
Preparing Digital Images for Printing, by Sybil Ihrig, Emil Ihrig, and Scott Rogers (Osborne/McGraw-Hill).
Real World Scanning and Halftones, by David Blatner, Glenn Fleishman, and Steve Roth (Peachpit Press).
The Rough Guide to the Internet, by Angus J. Kennedy (Rough Guides Ltd)

References
William J. Mitchell. *The Reconfigured Eye: Visual Truth in the Post-Photographic Era*. Cambridge, MA: MIT Press, 1992.
Martin Rieser. 'Art on the edge: Digital Printmaking Reviewed', in *Relativities: The 4th British International Miniature Print Exhibition*. Loughborough, UK: Loughborough University School of Art & Design, 2000.

SUPPLIES AND SERVICES

Digital Editioners/Printers
Adamson Editions, Washington DC, USA, http://www.adamsoneditions.com
Artificial Image, Berlin, Germany, http://www.artificialimage.com
Colville Place Gallery, London, UK, http://www.colvilleplacegallery.co.uk
Cone Editions Press, Vermont, USA, http://www.cone-editions.com
Hunter Editions, Maine, USA, http://www.huntereditions.com
Muse[X], Los Angeles, USA, http://www.musex.com
Nash Editions, California, USA, http://www.nasheditions.com
Sutton Atelier, Toronto, Canada, http://www.suttongraphics.com
Visualeyes Imaging Services, London, UK, http://www.visnet.co.uk

Hardware Manufacturers
Apple Computer, http://www.apple.com
Canon, scanners, printers, and other hardware, http://www.canon.com

EnCAD, large-format inkjet printers, http://www.encad.com
Epson, small- and large-format printers and other imaging hardware,
    http://www.epson.com
Hewlett-Packard, small- and large-format digital printers,
    http://www.hp.com
Iomega, Zip and Jaz drives, http://www.iomega.com
Iris Graphics, continuous inkjet printers, http://www.irisgraphics.com
Lexmark, inkjet printers and laser printers, http://www.lexmark.com
Tektronix, dye-sublimation and solid inkjet printers, http://www.tek.com
Umax, scanners, http://www.umax.com
Wacom, drawing tablets, http://www.wacom.com
(note: most printer manufacturers also supply ranges of specialist inks and
substrates – listed on their websites.)

Materials Suppliers
Compucolour, specialist inks and substrates, http://www.compucolor.com
Cone Editions Press, digital printmaking supplies,
    http://www.inkjetmall.com
Hahnemühle archival papers, http://www.digitalartsupplies.com
Hiromi, Japanese inkjet papers, http://www.hiromipaper.com
Hurst Chemical Company, laser plates for lithography,
    http://www.hurstchemical.com
Intaglio, specialist printmaking supplies, London, 020 7928 2633
John Purcell Papers, specialist printmaking papers,
    http://www.johnpurcell.net
T.N. Lawrence, specialist printmaking supplies, http://www.lawrence.co.uk
Lazertran, toner transfer papers, http://www.lazertran.com
Lyson, archival inks and papers, http://www.lyson.com
St Cuthberts Mills, Somerset papers, http://www.inveresk.co.uk

Software Producers
Adobe Systems, http://www.adobe.com
Autodessys, http://www.autodessys.com
Corel, http://www.corel.com
Macromedia, http://www.macromedia.com
MetaCreations, http://www.metacreations.com
Microsoft, http://www.microsoft.com
Quark, http://www.quark.com
Strata, http://www.strata.com

OTHER INFORMATION SOURCES

American Print Alliance, http://www.printalliance.org
Artbyte, magazine of digital culture, http://www.artbyteonline.com
Colville Place Gallery, http://www.colvilleplacegallery.co.uk
Digital Printmaker, http://www.digitalprintmaker.com
Fine Art Giclée Printers, http://www.fineartgicleeprinters.org
International Association of Fine Art Digital Printmakers (IAFADP),
    http://www.iafadp.org
The Kodak Digital Learning Centre, tutorials on digital imaging,
    http://www.kodak.com/US/en/digital/dlc
Wilhelm Imaging Research, materials testing, http://www.wilhelm-research.com

Algorithmic Art

Algorists, http://www.solo.com/studio/algorists.html
Evolutionary computation, http://www.red3d.com/cwr/evolve.html
Logo Foundation, http://el.www.media.mit.edu/logo-foundation/index.html
NPR (non-photorealistic rendering), http://www.red3d.com/cwr/npr
Shape grammars, http://www.shapegrammar.org
VRML Repository, http://www.web3d.org/vrml/vrml.htm

Art Online

Art on the Net, http://www.art.net
Britart, contemporary art sales, http://britart.com
Colville Place Gallery, http://www.colvilleplacegallery.co.uk
Digital Art Museum, http://www.dam.org
Eyestorm, contemporary art sales, http://www.eyestorm.com
The Gallery Online, http://www.galleryonline.com
GUILD.com, art marketing, http://www.guild.com
POD Gallery, online art store, http://www.podgallery.com

Web-based Art

Digital Mutations, http://www.digitalmutations.de
Generation/Mutation, http://www.digitalsouls.com
Peter Halley's Exploding Cell, http://www.moma.org/onlineprojects/halley/explodingcell.html

Maps of metal, Carinna Parraman, UK, 2001. Relief print on Somerset Velvet, with cotton muslin backing, 96 x 96 cm (37.8 x 37.8in.). Printed from a photo-polymer plate made from digital negatives.

INDEX